Gay and Lesbian Studies

The *Research on Homosexuality* series:

Series Editor: John P. De Cecco, PhD, Director, Center for Research and Education in Sexuality, San Francisco State University, and Editor, *Journal of Homosexuality*

Historical Perspectives on Homosexuality, edited by Sal Licata, PhD, and Robert P. Petersen, PhD candidate

Nature and Causes of Homosexuality: A Philosophic and Scientific Inquiry, edited by Noretta Koertge, PhD

Homosexuality & Psychotherapy: A Practitioner's Handbook of Affirmative Models, edited by John C. Gonsiorek, PhD

Alcoholism & Homosexuality, edited by Thomas O. Zeibold, PhD, and John Mongeon

Literary Visions of Homosexuality, edited by Stuart Kellogg

Homosexuality and Social Sex Roles, edited by Michael W. Ross, PhD

Bisexual and Homosexual Identities: Critical Theoretical Issues, edited by John P. De Cecco, PhD, and Michael G. Shively, MA

Bisexual and Homosexual Identities: Critical Clinical Issues, edited by John P. De Cecco, PhD

Homophobia: An Overview, edited by John P. De Cecco, PhD

Bisexualities: Theory and Research, edited by Fritz Klein, MD, and Timothy J. Wolf, PhD

Anthropology and Homosexual Behavior, edited by Evelyn Blackwood, PhD (cand.)

Historical, Literary, and Erotic Aspects of Lesbianism, edited by Monika Kehoe, PhD

Interdisciplinary Research on Homosexuality in the Netherlands, edited by A. X. van Naerssen

Psychotherapy with Homosexual Men and Women: Integrated Identity Approaches for Clinical Practice, edited by Eli Coleman, PhD

Psychopathology and Psychotherapy in Homosexuality, edited by Michael Ross, PhD

The Pursuit of Sodomy: Male Homosexuality in Renaissance and Enlightenment Europe, edited by Kent Gerard and Gert Hekma

Lesbians Over 60 Speak for Themselves, edited by Monika Kehoe

Gay and Lesbian Youth, edited by Gilbert Herdt

Homosexuality and the Family, edited by Frederick W. Bozett

Homosexuality and Religion, edited by Richard Hasbany, PhD

Love Letters Between a Certain Late Nobleman and the Famous Mr. Wilson, edited by Michael S. Kimmel, PhD

Male Intergenerational Intimacy: Historical, Socio-Psychological, and Legal Perspectives, edited by Theo Sandfort, PhD, Edward Brongersma, JD, and Alex van Naerssen, PhD

Gay Midlife and Maturity, edited by John Alan Lee, PhD

Gay People, Sex, and the Media, edited by Michelle A. Wolf, PhD, and Alfred P. Kielwasser, MA

Homosexuality and Male Bonding in Pre-Nazi Germany: The Youth Movement, the Gay Movement, and Male Bonding Before Hitler's Rise: Original Transcripts from Der Eigene, *The First Gay Journal in the World,* edited by Harry Oosterhuis, PhD, translations by Hubert Kennedy, PhD

Coming Out of the Classroom Closet: Gay and Lesbian Students, Teachers, and Curricula, edited by Karen M. Harbeck, PhD, JD

Homosexuality in Renaissance and Enlightenment England: Literary Representations in Historical Context, edited by Claude J. Summers, PhD

Gay and Lesbian Studies, edited by Henry L. Minton, PhD

This series is published by The Haworth Press, Inc., under the editorial auspices of the Center for Research and Education in Sexuality, San Francisco State University, and the *Journal of Homosexuality*.

Gay and Lesbian Studies has also been published as *Journal of Homosexuality*, Volume 24, Numbers 1/2 1992.

The Haworth Press, Inc., 10 Alice Street, Binghamton, NY 13904-1580 USA

Library of Congress Cataloging-in-Publication Data

Gay and lesbian studies / Henry L. Minton, editor.
     p. cm.
     "Originally published as Journal of homosexuality, volume 24, numbers 1/2, 1992"–CIP galley.
     Includes bibliographical references and index.
     ISBN 1-56024-307-4 (alk. paper)–ISBN 1-56023-021-5 (pbk. : alk. paper)
     1. Homosexuality–Study and teaching. I. Minton, Henry L.
HQ76.25.G377 1992
305.9'0664'07–dc20
                                   92-23738
                                      CIP

Gay and Lesbian Studies

Henry L. Minton, PhD
Editor

The Haworth Press, Inc.
New York • London • Norwood (Australia)

ABOUT THE EDITOR

Henry L. Minton, PhD, is Professor of Psychology at the University of Windsor. His research interests are in the history and theory of psychology and the psychological study of gay and lesbian issues. He has written articles on homosexual identity development, emancipatory social psychology as it relates to gay and lesbian issues, and the history of how homosexuality has been studied in American psychology and psychiatry. The latter topic is also treated in his biography, *Lewis M. Terman: Pioneer in Psychological Testing* (New York University Press, 1988).

Gay and Lesbian Studies

CONTENTS

∞ ALL HAWORTH BOOKS & JOURNALS
ARE PRINTED ON CERTIFIED
ACID-FREE PAPER

The Emergence of Gay and Lesbian Studies

Henry L. Minton, PhD

University of Windsor

Gay and lesbian studies is coming of age in the 1990s. As Ocamb (1990) points out, we are witnessing the same kind of enthusiasm that marked the establishment of black studies and women's studies in the 1970s.

A number of seminal developments have taken place in recent years. In 1986, a lesbian and gay studies center was created at Yale University. The Lesbian/Gay Studies Center at Yale is primarily a research center, and in 1987 it initiated an annual series of conferences on lesbian, bisexual, and gay issues. In the fall of 1990, the City University of New York Center for Lesbian and Gay Studies (CLAGS) was officially established as a research center. Academic programs are also emerging. The City College of San Francisco created the first gay and lesbian studies department at an American institution of higher education in 1988. Many universities in the United States and Canada are in the process of developing and/or expanding courses and programs in gay and lesbian studies. These pathbreaking events are by no means limited to North America. European universities were the first to institute academic programs. The most notable developments have taken place in The Netherlands, where gay and lesbian studies programs were initiated in the late 1970s.

At this critical juncture in the development of gay and lesbian

Henry L. Minton is Professor of Psychology at the University of Windsor. Correspondence may be addressed to the author at: Department of Psychology, University of Windsor, Windsor, Ontario, Canada N9B 3P4.

studies, this special volume is an attempt to provide a resource for the current state of the field. The contributions, therefore, represent a number of perspectives which should enlighten us about the nature of gay and lesbian studies, including historical and theoretical context, conceptual issues, the practicalities involved in teaching and developing programs, and political issues and implications. To some extent, this volume is similar to Margaret Cruikshank's (1982) pioneering sourcebook on lesbian studies. However, the scope here is enlarged to encompass both lesbian and gay studies as well as the issue of whether this is one integrated discipline or two separate ones.

In the history of Western thought, the scholarly study of same-sex love is but a recent footnote. While it is now possible to reclaim the gay and lesbian past, starting from its roots in the ancient world (see Duberman, Vicinus, & Chauncey, 1989), a gay intelligentsia did not become established until the nineteenth century (Adam, 1987). It was also within the nineteenth century that human sexuality in general, and homosexuality in particular, fell within the province of medicine and science (Weeks, 1985). While the early gay activists of the late nineteenth century coined the term "homosexuality" to identify and defend a form of sexual pluralism, the medical establishment and the sexologists, such as Krafft-Ebing and Freud, cited homosexuality as a form of sexual deviation. By the beginning of the twentieth century, the study of homosexuality was dominated by psychiatrists, psychoanalysts, and psychologists committed to a medical model of same-sex love as pathology. Within medical and scientific circles, it was Kinsey's (1948) *Sexual Behavior in the Human Male* which first challenged the medical model of pathology and alternatively advocated the position of homosexuality as an expression of sexual pluralism. The impact of the Kinsey studies, in terms of both challenging established scientific thought and raising public consciousness about homosexuality, is one of the historical forces that set the stage for the emergence of gay and lesbian studies. The Homophile movement of the 1950s and 1960s and, to an even greater extent, the post-Stonewall movements of Gay Liberation and Lesbian Feminism created the political climate for the early development of gay and lesbian studies in the 1970s. The growing sense of lesbian/gay community in response to the

AIDS crisis of the 1980s has undoubtedly played a role in the maturing of gay and lesbian studies as we move into the 1990s.

Jeffrey Escoffier takes us through the generational and intellectual shifts that have characterized the post-Stonewall movement of gay and lesbian studies. His historical and theoretical analysis underscores the way in which the personal experiences of being part of a generational cohort can shape intellectual and political worldviews. He also provides insight about the role of gender and race as shaping influences in the interpretation of lesbian and gay experience. His delineation of the five paradigms that form a conceptual foundation for gay and lesbian studies is especially useful as a point of reference for some of the positions taken by the other contributors to this volume.

Another aspect of the conceptual base for gay and lesbian studies is the issue of how we define the key terms we use. James Donovan deals with the problematics of defining *homosexual, homosexuality, gay,* and *lesbian.* He points out how the lack of both specificity and consensus surrounding these definitions confounds comparative research because the subject populations studied are often not consistent. Based on a sociolinguistic analysis of how these terms are used in real life situations, he makes recommendations about definitional boundaries.

The social construction of identity and cultural studies, two of the paradigms Escoffier delineates in his essay, provide the conceptual framework for ki namaste's examination of lesbian and gay studies as an interdisciplinary enterprise. Focusing on the theoretical and political strategy of deconstruction, namaste interprets interdisciplinary work as an interventionist practice within the academic community, which also has implications for societal change. Consistent with Donovan's suggestion that definitional boundaries cannot be separated from historical context, namaste stresses how lesbian and gay identities are socially constructed.

Like namaste, Arthur Flannigan-Saint-Aubin utilizes the cultural studies paradigm in his treatment of the interaction between the reader and the text. Perhaps, one of the most basic issues in gay and lesbian studies is the extent to which sexual identity affects how we interpret spoken and written discourse, as well as other forms of cultural codes and practices. Flannigan-Saint-Aubin deals specifically with male homosexuality and concludes that sexual identity plays a unique and central role in informing and structuring the reading of texts. Furthermore, he argues that the identification of a homosexual reading has political implications in that it constitutes a conscious act aimed at interpreting and changing the world.

The next set of contributions focuses on the experience and issues involved in teaching courses and developing programs in gay and lesbian studies. Joseph Cady draws on his experience in teaching gay and lesbian literature. He proposes that teaching such courses has a "subversive" value, or in other terms serves an emancipatory interest. The exposure to gay and lesbian content directly challenges the deep-seated cultural pressure to keep homosexuality "unspeakable" and "untouchable." We might say, in general, that courses in gay and lesbian studies substantially resist the invisibility of homosexuality, which has been a basic feature of gay oppression. Cady also argues that it is important for students to be exposed to the unique nature of gay oppression as it has existed historically, and he is critical of the social constructionist perspective which he feels negates the distinctiveness about homosexuality and its existence before the late nineteenth century.

Jack Collins tells the story of how the first Gay and Lesbian Studies Department at an American college or university was established and how it operates. This department was created in 1988 at the City College of San Francisco (CCSF) and offered its first courses in 1990. While there are lesbian and gay research centers at other universities, CCSF is still the only American institution of higher learning to have a Gay and Lesbian Studies Department. Two of Collins's colleagues, Margaret Cruikshank and Lindy McKnight, add their own statements about being associated with a Department of Gay and Lesbian Studies.

In contrast to the paucity of gay and lesbian studies programs in North America, a number of programs have developed in Europe. The Netherlands has been at the forefront of European developments. Gert Hekma and Theo van der Meer describe the development of gay and lesbian studies in The Netherlands, beginning with the founding of such programs in the late 1970s. They discuss the role of students and faculty in spearheading efforts to establish gay and lesbian studies, as well as the impact of the larger gay movement and Dutch society. As we might expect, breaking new ground is typically accompanied by internal tensions among those involved and we learn about the nature of gender relationships and inter-university competition. Based on a roundtable discussion of the current state of gay and lesbian studies in The Netherlands, Hekma and van der Meer also present a glimpse of future prospects.

The last two articles deal with special issues. The question of what lesbian studies is and how it relates to gay studies and women's studies is explored by Carolyn Gammon. She provides an overview of how lesbian studies has developed in Canada. She also draws on her own experience as a student who was instrumental in establishing a lesbian studies program at Concordia University in Montreal. Her student group developed the first series of lesbian studies courses in Canada. In her conclusion, she takes the position that lesbian studies should be developed as a distinct entity, that is independent from gay studies and women's studies. She also advocates that lesbian studies should be integrated into existing disciplines, with the aim of providing all students with the right to be exposed to a lesbian studies perspective as one of many perspectives.

As lesbian and gay studies becomes academically institutional-ized, there is the danger that it will lose its ties to the lesbian and gay political movement. Will Roscoe analyzes the role of commu-nity-based historians in reclaiming the lesbian and gay past. He identifies the ways in which these researchers have disseminated their research, specifically through the lesbian/gay archive, the slide-lecture presentation, and the community-based audience. These forms of communication nurture the construction of both knowledge and identity. It is therefore essential that academic scholars maintain links with the lesbian and gay community-based history movement.

In the Appendix of this issue, two excerpts are included from the published report of the Rutgers University committee for lesbian and gay concerns. This report, entitled *In Every Classroom*, serves as a model for articulating the connection between lesbian and gay studies and human rights concerns in institutions of higher learning. The goals and objectives of the report are contained in the Execu-tive Summary, the first of the two excerpts reprinted. Among the objectives presented is the need to integrate lesbian and gay studies into the existing teaching curricula. Such mainstreaming is viewed as crucial to combating homophobia and heterosexism.

The second excerpt from *In Every Classroom* is a representative bibliography of the kinds of books and articles which are relevant to the teaching of lesbian and gay studies. This is based on a survey of the teaching staff at Rutgers. While not meant to be a comprehensive reference list, it serves as a useful teaching resource for lesbian and gay studies. A more extensive bibliography is available in the second edition of Martin Duberman's (1991) book, *About Time*.

* * *

In bringing this volume to fruition, there were several individuals who generously provided me with suggestions and recommendations. I would like to acknowledge the help of Barry Adam, Dennis Altman, John De Cecco, Ruth Doell, Martin Duberman, Wayne Dynes, Gert Hekma, Dorelies Kraakman, John Alan Lee, Ron Nieberding, Claude Summers, Randolph Trumbach, Henk van den Boogaard, Theo van der Meer, and Jeri Wine.

REFERENCES

Adam, B. D. (1987). *The rise of a gay and lesbian movement.* Boston: Twayne.
Cruikshank, M. (Ed.). (1982). *Lesbian studies: Present and future.* Old Westbury, NY: Feminist Press.
Duberman, M. (1991). *About time: Exploring the gay past* (2nd ed.). New York: Dutton.
Duberman, M., Vicinus, M., & Chauncey, Jr., G. (Eds.). (1989). *Hidden from history: Reclaiming the gay and lesbian past.* New York: New American Library.
Kinsey, A. C., Pomeroy, W. B., & Martin, C. E. (1948). *Sexual behavior in the human male.* Philadelphia: Saunders.
Ocamb, K. (1990). Gay studies make the grade: How and where to find the lavender curriculum. *The Advocate*, No. 561, 40.
Weeks, J. (1985). *Sexuality and its discontents: Meanings, myths, and modern sexualities.* London: Routledge & Kegan Paul.

Generations and Paradigms: Mainstreams in Lesbian and Gay Studies

Jeffrey Escoffier

OUT/LOOK

SUMMARY. The development of lesbian and gay studies is traced from the Stonewell period of the late sixties and early seventies to the present. The effort to establish lesbian and gay studies has brought together several generations of scholars who have produced a variety of conceptual worldviews. These generational mainstreams of thought in lesbian and gay studies include the search for authenticity (1969-1976), the social construction of identity (1976-present), essential identity (1975-present), difference and race (1979-present), and cultural studies (1985-present).

The written word sounds like a pistol shot in many a closet. It is no surprise to most of us that literature, knowledge, and books about homosexuals have often served as the powerful tools of self-knowledge and acceptance for generations of gay men and lesbians. One has only to think of the historical role that *The Well of Loneliness*–despite all its flaws–has played for generations of lesbians, or that the "Calamus" poems of Walt Whitman had for male homosexuals like Oscar Wilde, J.A. Symonds, and Edward Carpenter in late nineteenth-century Britain, to realize the absolute significance of cultural and intellectual contributions to the emergence of the

Jeffrey Escoffier is the publisher of *OUT/LOOK: National Lesbian and Gay Quarterly*. He has taught lesbian and gay studies courses in sociology at the University of California, Berkeley. Correspondence may be addressed to the author at OUT/LOOK, 540 Castro Street, San Francisco, CA 94114.

modern homosexual.[1] The early days of the gay movement were full of intellectual ferment. Almost immediately after Stonewall a growing flood of books, periodicals and other publications found an eager audience who wanted to explore the political and cultural implications of lesbian feminism and gay liberation.

Over the last three or four years, concerted efforts to establish a lesbian and gay studies within the university have been underway at a number of institutions across North America–at Yale, The City University of New York, City College of San Francisco, MIT, Duke, University of Toronto, and a number of other campuses. These academic developments come on top of a recent boom in lesbian and gay publishing, both among small presses and commercial houses. Such developments are only possible with the solid growth of a sophisticated audience of lesbians and gay men who are interested in delving into the political and cultural issues of their lives. The creation of lesbian and gay studies sets the stage for a potentially significant historical shift in the intellectual life of the lesbian and gay communities–the entry of the university into the communities' cultural development.

BEGINNINGS: GENERATIONS, POLITICS AND COMMUNITY

Historical generations are not like families or political organizations, in which people are bound by kinship or commonly stated purposes. When a large group of people experiences significant historical events at the beginning of their adult life it often creates a sense of shared identity. While the demographic concept of "cohort" captures the idea of a group of people born at the same time, a generational identity is forged from a shared historical experience that creates a distinctive attitude toward life, a sensibility, and a collective state of mind.[2]

Generations in lesbian and gay life are more often characterized by the historical context of the time at which one *comes out* publicly than by closeness in chronological age. Important historical episodes like the Stonewall riots, the advent of AIDS (in which before or after is often the most significant aspect), or the influential political-cultural ideas of a period (lesbian-feminism between 1973-80 or the anti-porn debates of 1978-1984) define lesbian and gay generations. Together with the social and political challenges from outside the lesbian and gay communities these cultural trends are very important. In some sense, lesbian or gay "generations" are often of quite short duration (roughly five years) because of the swift pace of change in the political and cultural atmosphere. The Stonewall period of the late sixties and early seventies provided formative experiences for both women and men, although in somewhat different versions. Certainly the clash between the male-dominated gay liberation movement and lesbian-feminism deeply marked the women of the Stonewall generation. Lesbian-feminism created the context into which the next generation–the middle generation (i.e., the middle seventies)–of lesbians came out. Later the sex wars of the late seventies between the anti-pornography movement led by a number of lesbian-feminists and the feminist sex radicals established a new context into which women could come out. Now there is the post-sex war generation of lesbians. Gay male generations had a somewhat different rhythm. The lesbian separatist impulse of the mid-seventies left the men of the Stonewall generation isolated from the political debates of the women's movement. Nevertheless there is a middle generation of men who were decisively influenced–through women's studies courses and other public debates–by feminism. The sex wars stimulated intellectual exchanges between men on the gay left and the feminist sex radicals. The advent of AIDS created a major watershed in gay male, and to some degree lesbian, life. Many gay and lesbian sex radicals became involved in AIDS activism and education.

Lesbian and gay studies are not exempt from the historical circumstances that shape the political and cultural development of the lesbian and gay male communities. In the midst of the sweeping changes and waves of resistance to radical improvements in the lives of lesbians and gay men scholars, writers, and other intellectuals strive to formulate interpretations and theories of homosexual life that make sense, both of the historical changes and of the texture of everyday life. The intellectual frameworks or paradigms developed by scholars and community intellectuals reflect the underlying cultural assumptions of the times as well as suggesting concrete research programs. Research on lesbian and gay life takes place in most of the major disciplines of the humanities and social sciences, but a number of interdisciplinary theoretical paradigms have been very influential.

The recent effort to establish lesbian and gay studies brings together several generations of scholars. One is the generation of writers and scholars who experienced the euphoria of Stonewall and the women's movement in the early seventies. This generation has had to contend with the powerful cultural appeal for *personal authenticity*–the unrealized potentiality for self-cultivation, self-direction, self-understanding, and creativity.[3] But they have also had to struggle with the limits and anomalies of authenticity as a framework for research as well as a basis for social action. Important figures of this early generation are Jonathan Ned Katz, Esther Newton, John D'Emilio, Karla Jay, Lillian Faderman, John De Cecco, James Saslow, and Martin Duberman. The second wave has achieved its intellectual maturity under a different set of cultural assumptions–one much more attuned to the importance of cultural codes and the signifying practices. It is also still a world in which the appeal of authenticity has a place. This group of younger scholars weaves its way between these two perspectives; Eve Sedgewick, David Halperin, Diana Fuss, Thomas Yingling, Judith Butler, Douglas Crimp, and Michael Moon are representatives of this later generation. There is another group of writers and teachers–mostly women of color–who bridge these two generations and who have challenged lesbian and gay academics to confront the exclusion of race from intellectual and political discourse–among them are poet Audre Lorde, playwright Cherrie Moraga, editor and publisher Barbara Smith, and poet Gloria Anzaldua.

The work of each generation has markedly different intellectual styles. The Stonewall generation has created three influential intellectual perspectives that have framed research in lesbian and gay studies–a social-psychological model of authentic selfhood, the social constructionist theory of homosexual identity, and essentialist theories of the woman-identified lesbian identity and of gay identity. These three paradigms are linked together in their struggle to articulate the dialectic of authenticity and history. The later generation has emerged from literary and cultural criticism; it has developed an eclectic approach that emphasizes the significance of inter-pretative strategies and cultural codes in gay and lesbian life. The paradigm articulated by Audre Lorde, Cherrie Moraga, Gloria An-zaldua, and Barbara Smith is rooted in the discovery of authentic selfhood but it explores the effects of hegemonic social patterns on the constitution of social and personal identities. It challenges the exclusion of difference and race from the approaches of the two generations.

Of course, some scholars do not seem to fit exactly into any generational grouping–such as historian John Boswell or film theo-rist Teresa de Laurentis. One group of Stonewall generation schol-ars under the leadership of Wayne Dynes has not worked within these paradigms but instead worked on series of projects that culmi-nated in the publication of the *Encyclopedia of Homosexuality* in 1990. But all of these groups inhabit a growing niche in academic life–the lesbian and gay studies program.

THE SEARCH FOR AUTHENTICITY, 1969-1976

The generation of lesbians and gay men galvanized by Stonewall had already witnessed five tumultuous years of intense political activity that fundamentally challenged American values–black civil rights, the student anti-war movement, the women's movement, and the emergence of the counterculture. The cultural atmosphere was ringing with ideas of Black Power, sexual revolution, and liberation. Many of the leading intellectual figures of the period promoted sexual liberation–Herbert Marcuse, Paul Goodman, James Baldwin, Susan Sontag, Allen Ginsberg. Goodman, Baldwin, and Ginsberg were openly homosexual, and in *Eros and Civilization* Marcuse had explicitly nominated homosexuals as cultural revolutionaries. In *The Second Sex* Simone de Beauvoir had written the first major feminist work of the postwar era and in a string of influential books and essays like *Jew and Anti-Semite, Saint Genet,* the Preface to Franz Fanon's *The Wretched of the Earth,* and his chapters in *Being and Nothingness* on the authenticity and bad faith of the homosexual, Jean-Paul Sartre explored the psychology of authentic identity.[4] This generation grounded its thinking in its own existential experience of socially-repressed homosexual desire against the more naturalist Freudian presumption of universal bisexuality. The impulse towards realizing one's authentic self informed much of the thinking and action of the political and cultural movements of the sixties. The experience of "coming out"–so fundamental to the personal and political development of gay and lesbian identities–is a perfect illustration of an individual's experience of authentic selfhood. Sartre, Beauvoir, Paul Goodman, and others who wrote on the importance of being true to one's authentic self were often the intellectual sources that influenced lesbian and gay writers, intellectuals, and young academics when they took up writing about gay liberation and feminism. The emphasis on authenticity and identity grew out of a reaction to the Freudian assumption of bisexuality which was prevalent among prominent writers of the previous generation–Tennessee Williams, Lorraine Hansbury, Gore Vidal, James Baldwin. Two of the most influential works that framed a great deal of the early writing on lesbian and gay studies were Dennis Altman's *Homosexual: Oppression and Liberation* and Kate Millett's *Sexual Politics*. Both authors drew on the search for authenticity as a framework for their analysis of sexual oppression and liberation, yet both were still committed to Freudian ideas about the "polymorphous perversity" and bisexuality of human desire.[5]

Almost immediately after Stonewall a growing flood of books, periodicals, and other publications found an eager audience who wanted to explore the political and cultural implications of lesbian feminism and gay liberation. The powerful lesbian-feminist essay "The Woman-Identified Woman" was published in 1970. Then a year later Dennis Altman published *Homosexual: Oppression and Liberation*, the first post-Stonewall book on the politics of gay liberation. In the same year Donn Teal published *The Gay Militants*, the first history of the American homophile and gay movements. It was followed by Kay Tobin's *The Gay Crusaders* in 1972. Between 1972 and 1978 Karla Jay and Allan Young published a series of anthologies (*Out of the Closets, After You're Out, Lavender Culture*) that explored gay and lesbian history, psychological theories, the problems and possibilities of coming out, lesbian and gay culture before and after Stonewall, the gay movement's relation to the left, the women's movement and the black civil rights movement, sex roles, the images of gay men and lesbians in the media.[6]

The Stonewall generation made an effort to bring the gay liberation and feminist perspectives to bear on their research and writing when they founded the Gay Academic Union in March 1973. Martin Duberman, Bertha Harris, Karla Jay, John D'Emilio, Jonathan Ned Katz, and Barbara Gittings were among those involved. This group held its first conference on November 23 and 24 of that year. Three hundred people attended that first conference at John Jay College of Criminal Justice of the City University of New York. After that GAU organized two other conferences in New York before political divisions broke up the group and the annual conference moved out to Los Angeles where it acquired an emphasis on psychotherapy and a broader cultural purpose.

GAU grew out of a need to confront the virulent homophobia of academia. But from the very beginning this early attempt to create a place for lesbian and gay studies also had to contend with the institutionalized gender imbalance of the university system. All of GAU's activities were entangled in the tensions between men and women. The organization was overwhelmingly male in membership and the few women who attended meetings were constantly put in the awkward position of challenging recurring sexist comments and the underlying chauvinism of their male colleagues. GAU did publish a political statement of purpose that listed opposition to all forms of discrimination against women within academia as the first priority, and opposition to all forms of discrimination against gay people as second.[7] Nevertheless all three conferences in New York were marked by increasingly bitter confrontations between lesbians and gay men.

Mixed in the tensions between lesbians and gay men was another conflict about the relation between politics and scholarship. Some members of GAU argued that value of scholarship and academic debate was not affected by male chauvinism. Splits also developed among gay men over their stances towards lesbian-feminist criticism of gay male academics. The divisions among the men were exacerbated because they occurred along lines of left versus right. By

1975 the radical men and most lesbians left GAU, the conferences moved to Los Angeles while Wayne Dynes and his colleagues kept GAU in New York going for several years.[8]

The rapid growth of women's studies programs in the seventies often provided a safe space for lesbian studies–that is, courses with lesbian content and themes. During the following years women's and gay caucuses were formed in a number of academic profession-al associations like the Modern Language Association (for teachers of language and literature), the American Sociological Association, American Psychological Association, American Anthropological Association, the American Historical Association, and a few others. The professional association caucuses became the arena where both openly gay and closeted academics could meet and discuss research on homosexual themes as well as deal with job and research biases within the professions.

And in institutions across the country, in small liberal colleges, big state schools, and at elite universities openly gay and lesbian teachers taught courses in their departments that dealt either exclu-sively or in passing with homosexuality. In addition many courses were initiated and taught by the students themselves with the help of a friendly faculty sponsor.

One of the earliest academic fields to experience this infusion of energy was literature. Right around the same time that teachers and writers were meeting in New York to start GAU Louie Crew and Rictor Norton, a Professor of English and a literary critic, were putting together a special issue of *College English* on "The Homo-sexual Imagination." The introduction to the issue was called, "The Homophobic Imagination."[9] The special issue fed the rediscovery of lesbian and gay writers of the past: Isherwood, Vita Sackville-West, Jean Genet, Gertrude Stein and Alice Toklas, Radcliffe Hall. Mass market paperback editions of many lesbian and gay authors were reissued during the 1970s.

The search for authenticity underlay the impulse that led gay and lesbian scholars to track down the history of homosexuals. The political significance of black history, the new leftist idea of "histo-ry from the bottom up," and the feminist motto "the personal is the political" provided the basis for a new approach to social history. In 1971 gay activist Jonathan Ned Katz started doing research on gay history, starting only from the presumption that gay American history actually existed. In June 1972 he mounted a dramatization of some of his early discoveries in a documentary play "Coming Out" modeled on Martin Duberman's successful off-Broadway play, "In White America."[10] Eventually his research led to two huge collections of lesbian and gay historical documents, *Gay American History*, published in 1976, and in 1983 *Gay/Lesbian Almanac*. In the meantime Katz had served as the general editor of the Arno Press (then a division of The New York Times Co.) series "Homosexuality: Lesbians and Gay Men in Society, History, and Literature" a massive reprinting of over 100 books, from classics to the obscure, dealing with homosexuality from the nineteenth-century to the twentieth-century. Also in the early seventies, John D'Emilio and James Steakley, graduate students in history and German literature as well as gay activists, published in the Canadian gay journal *The Body Politic* pioneering explorations of the pre-Stonewall homosexual emancipation movements during the 1940s and 1950s in the United States and in pre-Nazi Germany. Eventually their work was published in book form. In 1974 John Lauritsen and David Thorstad published their short survey of pre-Stonewall political history, *The Early Homosexual Rights Movement (1864-1935)*.

The publication of Jonathan Ned Katz' *Gay American History* in 1976 was the culmination of the early tradition of lesbian and gay scholarship that worked within the loose intellectual paradigm rooted in the search for authenticity.[11] Ambiguities in the idea of the homosexual identity emerged from the inclusion in *Gay American History* of *berdache*, that is, men who adopted the female role in Native American societies and engaged in sexual activities with their husbands, of passionate friendships between pairs of men and women who probably did not engage in sexual activity with each other, and of women who chose to pass and live as men who may or may not have had homoerotic desires. Most of these people did not seem to resemble "homosexuals" as we knew ourselves. These ambiguities raised questions about who was "a homosexual" in earlier historical periods and in different cultures. Once scholars and

writers raised these questions the idea of discovering the history of
authentic homosexuals seemed problematic. It was precisely these
questions that stimulated the emergence of a new paradigm.

THE SOCIAL CONSTRUCTION OF IDENTITY, 1976-PRESENT

The outpouring of lesbian and gay social thought and history in
the early 1970s assumed that the homosexual experience in earlier
periods of history and in different cultures all revealed a type of
human personality called "the homosexual." But lesbian and gay
historians found increasingly that homosexual activity frequently
occurred without the presence of "homosexuals" and that intense
homosocial or erotic relationships existed between people who
otherwise did not appear to be "homosexuals." One solution to
these puzzles already had been ventured by British sociologist Mary
McIntosh. Her scholarly paper on "The Homosexual Role" had
been published in an American academic journal called *Social
Problems* in 1968–even before Stonewall. Challenging the belief
that there are two kinds of people in the world: "homosexuals" and
"heterosexuals," McIntosh argued that the homosexual should be
seen as a social role rather than as a condition. She expanded her
argument by explaining that the "role" of homosexual did not
simply describe a pattern of sexual behaviour but also other kinds
of cultural activities.[12]

The historical and political implications of McIntosh's theory was
worked out by a group of young British intellectuals in the journal
Gay Left (1975-1979). In the pages of their journal they created a
synthesis of Marxist social history and the "symbolic inter-
actionist" school of sociology–which emphasized the importance of
socially created meanings in everyday life.[13] This perspective on
the historical emergence of the homosexual identity informed
Jeffrey Week's *Coming Out: Homosexual Politics in Britain from
the Nineteenth Century to the Present* published in 1977. The Gay
Left writers elaborated on the making of the modern homosexual in
a series of essays that has been collected in two anthologies: *Homo-*

sexuality: *Power and Politics* (1980) edited by the Gay Left Collective and in *The Making of the Modern Homosexual* (1981) edited by Kenneth Plummer. The work of John D'Emilio brings together this new theory of homosexual identity and the new social history exemplified by his book *Sexual Politics, Sexual Communities*: *The Making of a Homosexual Minority in the United States, 1940-1970*.[14] This approach to gay history was eventually identified as the social constructionist theory of homosexual identity. While the early emphasis on authenticity was built on the catharsis of coming out, social constructionism reflected the discursive formation of lesbian and gay selfhood–it offered a grand narrative of historical progress.

French historian Michel Foucault's *History of Sexuality* (1978) offered a similar account of the historical creation of the homosexual identity.[15] But Foucault's work also presented a full-scaled philosophical critique of essentialism–the belief that "the homosexual identity" exists throughout history. Most of us start out as essentialists–that is, when we first come out, we believe that Socrates and Sappho were "homosexuals" in the same way that lesbians or gay men of the late twentieth-century are homosexuals. This belief is the naive form of essentialism. Lesbian and gay studies emerged from the essentialist impulse–the search for authenticity and roots–but the debate on the historical and social construction of the homosexual identity has increasingly framed the issues that have been addressed by lesbian and gay scholars.

The social constructionist theory of sexuality and sexual identity played an important role in the political debates on pornography in the late 1970s and early 1980s. The anti-pornography movement and the work of its leading theorists, Andrea Dworkin, Susan Griffin, Adrienne Rich, Audre Lourde, and Catherine MacKinnon often drew upon essentialist definitions of gender. Critics of the anti-pornography movement such as Carole Vance, Gayle Rubin, Amber Hollibaugh, Ellen Willis, Joan Nestle, Deirdre English, and Cherrie Moraga were social constructionists. The political and intellectual debates on sexuality and feminism surfaced in a controversial conference at Barnard College in 1982. The papers from this conference were later published in an influential anthology called *Pleasure and*

Danger: *Exploring Female Sexuality*, edited by the conference organizer, Carole Vance.[16] This together with another anthology, *Powers of Desire*, edited by Ann Snitow, Christine Stansell, and Sharon Thompson, made major contributions to social constructionist thinking about sexuality, gender, and sexual identity.

But the social constructionist theory of homosexual identity has its own ambiguities–specific sexual identities co-exist with evidence that sexual behavour appears to be a continuum, and seems to vary over the life cycle, and homosexual–identified individuals seem to exist in societies before the making of the modern homosexual identity took place. Some of these ambiguities were explored by Steven Epstein in an influential essay, "Gay Politics, Ethnic Identity: The Limits of Social Constructionism" and by Diana Fuss in the chapter on "The Question of Identity Politics" in her book *Essentially Speaking*.[17] Despite the theory's ambiguities and limits, the development of a social constructionist interpretation of homosexual history is one of the major intellectual achievements of the Stonewall generation of lesbian and gay scholars.

ESSENTIAL IDENTITY: LESBIAN EXISTENCE AND GAY UNIVERSALS, 1975-PRESENT

Lesbian-feminism was the most thoroughly developed political philosophy to emerge from the heady days of early feminism and gay liberation. First publically articulated in the pamphlet "The Woman-Identified Woman" published by Radicalwomen and Jill Johnston's *Lesbian Nation,* it also provided a framework for a sophisticated body of feminist scholarship. Authors like Mary Daly, Kathleen Barry, Susan Griffin, Diana Russell, Catherine MacKinnon, Lillian Faderman, and Adrienne Rich developed bold and vigorous interpretations of feminist politics, pornography, rape, lesbian culture, theology, and history. Lesbian-feminist scholarship worked with the presupposition that male and female behavior was "essentially" different, politically opposed, and not very amenable to change. Patriarchy was seen as a trans-historical outcome of the male domination of women by means of compulsory heterosexuality. Among the most important theoretical essays within this paradigm were two essays published in the early eighties in *Signs,* Adrienne Rich's "Compulsory Heterosexuality and Lesbian Existence" and Catherine MacKinnon's "Feminism, Marxism, Method and The State."[18] While lesbian-feminism theory presupposed that gender was immutable, it did argue that heterosexuality was socially constructed. Its "essentialist" notion of gender was very important to the thinking of the anti-pornography movement in the late seventies and early eighties–particularly in the work of Susan Griffin, Andrea Dworkin, and Catherine MacKinnon. If the early emphasis on authenticity reflected the coming out experience, and social constructionism captured the discursive aspects of identity development, lesbian-feminism synthesized growing revulsion toward male misogyny and the appeal of women's separatism. Lesbian-feminism was both a continuation of the search for authenticity-though in this case an authentic female identity–and a theory of the social construction of heterosexuality. The rejection of heterosexuality and the acceptance of lesbian identity led to an authentic women's culture.

The existence of gay or lesbian identities throughout history and in different cultures is the basis of another variant of "essentialism." In some versions it remains a relatively naive form of essentialism or even more crudely–hunting for "famous homosexuals."[19] In other versions it is relatively sophisticated. John Boswell and Will Roscoe have each published important theoretical statements of an interpretation of gay history that finds universal components of homosexual identities.[20] A number of these versions of history are often rooted in the history of religion. The earliest version of the "new essentialism" was published by Arthur Evans in *Fag Rag,* the radical political newspaper, and then in book form, *Witchcraft and the Gay Counterculture.* There Evans linked the persecution of gay people to the repression of the pagan witches. This book became an important source for the fairy movement, the movement of gay male spirituality. John Boswell's history of "gay people" in the middle ages, *Christianity, Social Tolerance and Homosexuality* (1980), portrayed a more tolerant Christianity and gave the "new essentialism" academic respectability. Judy Grahn applied her skills as a poet and storyteller in a book called *Another Mother Tongue* (1984) to provide a unique brew of history, etymology, and fiction.

While the lesbian-feminist paradigm and the very different versions of gay universalism of Boswell, Evans, and Grahn assume certain essential gender or sexual identities they also assume that other aspects are socially constructed. The essentialist paradigm implies that research in lesbian and gay studies must focus on realities or structures that span across historical periods–patriarchy, spiritual identities, or the basis of sexual or gender identities in nature.

DIFFERENCE AND RACE: 1979-PRESENT

Within the women's movement a new group of writers emerged to challenge what Adrienne Rich called the movement's "white solipsism"–its tendency "to think, imagine, and speak as if whiteness described the world."[21] In a number of important speeches and essays Audre Lorde criticized feminists' refusal to include differences of race and class in their analysis of male domination.[22] The major contribution to a new exploration of the discourse and expression of multifaceted/multicultural identities was made by the anthology *This Bridge Called My Back*, edited by Cherrie Moraga and Gloria Anzaldua. The writers in this tradition have examined the faultlines and borders on which women of color have built their identities–the change in generation between mother and daughter, the language barriers, sexual identities, the specific cultural histories of different races, the physical bodies of women of color, and the diversity of work situations.[23] The important breakthrough of *This Bridge Called My Back* was followed up by other anthologies such as *Home Girls: A Black Feminist Anthology* (1983), edited by Barbara Smith, Gloria Anzaldua's sequel to her book with Cherrie Moraga, *Making Face, Making Soul/Hacienda Caras* (1990), and Carla Trujilla's *Chicana Lesbians* (1991). Gloria Anzaldua and Cherrie Moraga have both written in-depth autobiographical profiles of the multifaceted bridge identities of women of color. Gloria Anzaldua explores her identity as "a border woman" in *Borderlands/La Frontera* (1987). She maps the psychological, sexual, and spiritual borderlands of her life in a work that switches "codes" from English to Castillian Spanish, North Mexican dialect, Tex-

Mex, and even Nahuatl. Cherrie Moraga takes up a similar exploration in *Loving in the War Years/Lo que nunca paso por sus labios*
(1983).

The contribution of *This Bridge Called My Back* and the intellectual framework that it established to lesbian and gay studies is the
mapping of those identities that exist at the juncture of different
cultures and different races. Gay male writers and scholars are just
beginning to explore this terrain.[24] Essex Hemphill has completed
an anthology of essays and other work that analyzes the bridge
identities of black gay men.[25] Lesbian and gay studies, like the
dominant American culture, must avoid ''white solipsism'' in order
to understand the diversity of lesbian and gay life.

IN PURSUIT OF SIGNS: THE CULTURAL STUDIES PARADIGM, 1985-PRESENT

The new generation of lesbian and gay scholars is explicitly
building on the work of the social construction of identity paradigm
and extending it to include the interpretation of all kinds of texts,
cultural codes, signifying practices, and modes of discourse that
shape underlying social attitudes towards homosexuality as well as
the formation of sexual or gender identities. As one member of the
new generation, Thomas Yingling, has noted, ''gay writers seem
often to have found literature less a matter of self-expression and
more a matter of coding.''[26] The gay absorption into signs, meanings, interpretation, and art is related to the fact that for the homosexual the 'problem of the homosexual' is in fact the problem of
signs—homosexuality is a semiotic. This intellectual shift in lesbian
and gay studies is led by scholars who began writing on lesbian and
gay issues in the wake of the sex debates of the late seventies and
early eighties. The new generation of lesbian and gay scholars is
influenced by academic developments like ''the New Historicism''
and what is increasingly called cultural studies—an interdisciplinary
synthesis of fields of study such as American studies, ethnic studies,
gender studies, and so on. Their intellectual framework is derived
from literary studies and the humanities and influenced by cultural
theorists like Roland Barthes, Michel Foucault, Mikhail Bakhtin,

Antonio Gramsci, Victor Turner, and Clifford Geertz.[27] Representatives of this new approach are Eve Kosovsky Sedgwick, who has explored male homosexuality and homosocial desire in literature; Thomas Yingling, author of an original study of Hart Crane; Judith Butler, a philosopher who has published a book on the theory of gender identity; David Miller, author of a well-received book on the police in the Victorian novel; David Halperin, who has pioneered a new interpretation of homosexuality in ancient Greece; Diana Fuss, author of a collection of essays on essentialism and identity politics; Michael Moon, who has written on Walt Whitman; and Lee Edelman, who has published a string of brilliant papers on gay literature including a famous essay on "Silence = Death."[28]

In an important theoretical statement of the cultural studies paradigm Harold Beaver wrote:

> The homosexual is beset by signs, by the urge to interpret whatever transpires, between himself and chance acquaintance. He is a prodigious consumer of signs–of hidden meanings, hidden systems, hidden potentiality. Exclusion from the common code impels the frenzied quest: the momentary glimpse, the scrambled figure, the chance encounter, the reverse image, the sudden slippage, the lowered guard. In a flash meanings may be disclosed, mysteries wrenched out and betrayed.[29]

Eve Sedgewick's recent *Epistemology of the Closet* is a major statement of the cultural studies paradigm. In it she argues that "an understanding of virtually any aspect of modern Western culture must be, not merely incomplete, but damaged in its central substance to the degree that does not incorporate a critical analysis of modern homo/heterosexual definition. . . ."[30]

The political implications of this model of cultural analysis have been heatedly debated. In her book *Gender Trouble* Judith Butler has "attempted to locate the political in the very signifying practices that establish, regulate, and deregulate identity."[31] The practical working out of this approach is clearly demonstrated by the work of cultural activists on AIDS, especially groups of artists, video and filmmakers. This work of propaganda, education, and media criticism displays great sophistication about the cultural codes of sexual behaviour, disease, and politics.[32]

THE FUTURE OF LESBIAN AND GAY STUDIES

While all five paradigms continue to have loyal adherents whose research and writing follow from presuppositions of the theories that constitute the core exemplars of the paradigms, lesbian and gay studies is divided by the different cultural styles of various generations. Many of the Stonewall generation retain their commitment to the twin problematics of authenticity and history—whether they are social constructionists or essentialists. Only the authenticity line of thought has not produced a major work of synthesis with a claim to represent an authoritative understanding of lesbian and gay life. The post-Stonewall generation came of age in a culture dominated by mass media and is acutely aware of the power of cultural codes. As post-Stonewall scholars enter the ranks of academics the cultural studies paradigm has become increasingly influential. It is a flexible and eclectic framework that can incorporate elements from some of the other paradigms, but it also is stylistically more difficult and less accessible than most of the work that is produced in the other research traditions. It runs the chance that it may lose the audience of readers and intellectuals in the community that have been the most supportive audience of the work written by scholars committed to the other frameworks.

NOTES

1. Although this belief has long been central to my thinking about the cultural politics of lesbian and gay life I owe this sharp formulation to Ara Wilson. On the significance of *The Well of Loneliness* see Esther Newton, "The Mythic Mannish Lesbian: Radclyffe Hall and the New Woman" *Signs*, Vol. 9, No. 4 (Summer, 1984); on the impact of Whitman on Wilde, Symonds, and Carpenter see Jeffrey Weeks, *Coming Out: Homosexual Politics in Britain from the Nineteenth Century to the Present* (London: Quartet Books, 1977), pp. 45-83.

2. See the essays by Karl Mannheim, "The Problem of Generations," in *Essays on the Sociology of Knowledge*, ed. Paul Kecskemeti (New York: Oxford University Press, 1952); Annie Kriegel, "Generational Difference: The History of

an Idea,'' *Daedalus, Proceedings of the American Academy of Arts and Sciences*, Vol. 107, No. 4 (Fall, 1978), pp. 23-38; and Matilda White Riley, ''Ageing, Social Change and the Power of Ideas,'' *Daedalus, Proceedings of the American Academy of Arts and Sciences*, Vol. 107, No. 4 (Fall, 1978), pp. 39-52; for an excellent example of generational history see Robert Wohl, *The Generation of 1914* (Cambridge, MA: Harvard University Press, 1979).

3. For two opposing testimonials on the significance of this issue see Marshall Berman, *The Politics of Authenticity: Radical Individualism and the Emergence of Modern Society* (New York: Atheneum, 1974), and Lionel Trilling, *Sincerity and Authenticity* (Cambridge, MA: Harvard University Press, 1971).

4. For a critical discussion of the model implicit in this approach see Frederick A. Olafson, ''Authenticity and Obligation,'' in Mary Warnock, ed., *Sartre: A Collection of Critical Essays* (New York, Doubleday Anchor Books, 1971), pp. 121-175.

5. Dennis Altman, *Homosexual: Oppression and Liberation* (New York: Outerbridge & Dienstfrey, 1971), and Kate Millet, *Sexual Politics* (New York: Doubleday & Co., 1970).

6. An anniversary edition of Karla Jay and Allen Young, *Out of the Closets*, is due out from New York University Press.

7. *The Universities and the Gay Experience* (New York: Gay Academic Union, 1974).

8. Under Wayne Dynes' leadership the GAU published a series on monographs including his *Homolexis: A Historical and Cultural Lexicon of Homosexuality* (New York: Gay Academic Union, Gai Sabor Monograph #4, 1985). Dynes was the editor of *Homosexuality: A Research Guide* (New York: Garland Publishing, Inc, 1987) and the *Encyclopedia of Homosexuality* (New York: Garland Publishing Inc., 1990).

9. ''The Homosexual Imagination,'' *College English*, Vol. 36, No. 3 (November, 1974).

10. Interview with Jonathan Katz, *The Gay Alternative*, No. 6 (1974).

11. Jonathan [Ned] Katz, *Gay American History* (New York: Thomas Y. Crowell Co., 1976).

12. Mary McIntosh, ''The Homosexual Role''; reprinted in Kennneth Plummer, *The Making of the Modern Homosexual* (London: Hutchinson, 1981). In the same volume see also the interview with Mary McIntosh, pp. 44-49.

13. The work of Erving Goffman explored the discursive formation of identities and social interaction. See Erving Goffman, *Stigma* (Englewood Cliffs, NJ: Prentice-Hall, Inc., 1963).

14. John D'Emilio, ''Capitalism and Gay Identity,'' Ann Snitow, Christine Stansell & Sharon Thompson, eds., *Powers of Desire: The Politics of Sexuality* (New York: Monthly Review Press, 1983); John D'Emilio, *Sexual Politics, Sexual Communities: The Making of a Homosexual Minority in the United States, 1940-1970* (Chicago: University of Chicago Press, 1983).

15. Michel Foucault, *The History of Sexuality, Volume I: An Introduction* (New York: Pantheon Books, 1978).

16. Carole Vance, ed., *Pleasure and Danger: Exploring Female Sexuality* (New York: Routledge, 1984).

17. Steven Epstein, "Gay Politics, Ethnic Identity: The Limits of Social Constructionism," *Socialist Review*, No. 93/94, Vol. 17, Nos 3-4 (May-August 1987); and Diana Fuss, *Essentially Speaking: Feminism, Nature and Difference*, (New York: Routledge, 1989).

18. Adrienne Rich "Compulsory Heterosexuality and Lesbian Existence," *Signs*, Vol. 5, No. 4 (1980), and Catherine MacKinnon "Feminism, Marxism, Method and The State," *Signs*, Vol. 7, No.3, (1982).

19. A.L. Rowse, *Homosexuals in History: Ambisexuals in Society, Literature and the Arts* (New York: Macmillan & Co. 1977).

20. John Boswell, "Revolutions, Universals, and Sexual Categories" *Salmagundi*, Nos. 58-59 (Fall 1982-Winter 1983); Will Roscoe "Making History: The Challenge of Gay and Lesbian Studies," *Journal of Homosexuality*, Vol. 15, Nos. 3/4 (1988).

21. Adrienne Rich, "Disloyal to Civilization: Feminism, Racism, Gynephobia," in *On Lies, Secrets and Silence* (New York: W.W. Norton, 1979), pp. 229.

22. Audre Lorde, *Sister Outsider: Essays and Speeches* (Trumansberg, NY: The Crossing Press, 1984).

23. Cherrie Moraga and Gloria Anzaldua, eds., *This Bridge Called My Back* (New York: Kitchen Table Press, 1981), pp. 105-106. See also Norma Alarcon, "The Theoretical Subject(s) of *This Bridge Called My Back* and Anglo-American Feminism," in Gloria Anzaldua, *Making Face, Making Soul/Hacienda Caras* (San Francisco: Aunt Lute Foundation Book, 1990).

24. Tomas Almaguer, "Chicano Men: A Cartography of Homosexual Identity And Behaviour," in *Differences: A Journal of Feminist Cultural Studies*, Vol. 3, No. 2 (Summer, 1991).

25. Essex Hemphill, ed., *Brother To Brother: An Anthology of Writings by Black Gay Men* (Boston: Alyson Publications, 1991).

26. Thomas E. Yingling, *Hart Crane and the Homosexual Text* (Chicago: University of Chicago Press, 1990), p. 25.

27. For background on these developments see Patrick Brantlinger, *Crusoe's Footprints: Cultural Studies in Britain and America* (New York: Routledge, 1990), and H. Aram Veeser, ed., *The New Historicism* (New York: Routledge, 1989).

28. A good sampling of work of this new generation can be found in an anthology entitled *Displacing Homophobia*, edited by Ronald R. Butters, John M. Clum, and Michael Moon (Durham: Duke University Press, 1990).

29. Harold Beaver, "Homosexual Signs (In Memory of Roland Barthes)" *Critical Inquiry*, Vol. 8, No. 1 (Autumn 1981), p. 104.

30. Eve Kosofsky Sedgwick, *Epistemology of the Closet* (Berkeley: University of California Press, 1990), p. 1.

31. Judith Butler, *Gender Trouble: Feminism and the Subversion of Identity* (New York: Routledge, 1990), pp. 147-149.

32. See Douglas Crimp with Adam Rolston, *AIDS DEMO GRAPHICS* (Seattle: Bay Press, 1990); Douglas Crimp, ed., *AIDS: Cultural Analysis, Cultural Activism* (Cambridge, MA: MIT Press, 1989); Tessa Boffin and Sunil Gupta, eds., *Ecstatic Antibodies* (London: Rivers Oram Press, 1990).

Homosexual, Gay, and Lesbian: Defining the Words and Sampling the Populations

James M. Donovan, PhD (cand.)

Tulane University

SUMMARY. The lack of both specificity and consensus about definitions for *homosexual, homosexuality, gay,* and *lesbian* are first shown to confound comparative research and cumulative understanding because criteria for inclusion within the subject populations are often not consistent. The Description section examines sociolinguistic variables which determine patterns of preferred choice of terminology, and considers how these might impact gay and lesbian studies. Attitudes and style are found to influence word choice. These results are used in the second section to devise recommended definitional limits which would satisfy both communication needs and methodological purposes, especially those of sampling.

To study gays and lesbians is to study whom? The response to this question will determine both the success and the value of "gay and lesbian studies." Inconsistent responses, however, make it unsurprising for workers to reach contradictory conclusions if, upon examination, they are dealing with different populations albeit labeled by the same terms (cf. Gorsky, 1981, p. 269).

Just what are the defining attributes which sort out the focal

James M. Donovan is a graduate student in the anthropology department of Tulane University. Correspondence may be addressed to: 1021 Audubon, New Orleans, LA 70118. Thanks are due to Judith M. Maxwell and Stephen O. Murray for critiques of earlier drafts of this paper, and to Jorge Vasconez for his support and patience.

27

phenomena for gay and lesbian studies? Is the group glossed by the morpheme *homosexual*, or those by *gay* and *lesbian*, sufficiently homogeneous between researchers to be treated as representatives of a single universe (cf. Stoller, 1980)? The issue is pivotal because it determines who is a suitable subject for which study.

Random sampling is the ideal method to choose subjects when the goal is to generalize about a larger population (Chambliss & Dunlap, 1977). Critical to the process are first to define the boundaries of the category (structuring the universe), and second to identify all members of the category (populating the universe). Students of homosexuality concede that Identification is practically impossible due to the hidden nature of the homosexual population (Bell & Weinberg, 1978). Instead of drawing samples randomly from the complete universe, we are obliged to take them from the most accessible sources (e.g., bars and, in the past, prisoners and patients), knowing them to be probably skewed relative to the broader homosexual population for at least some variables (Gonsiorek, 1982).

The comforting assumption has been that if members of this population could only be more exhaustively "catalogued," samples would be more random, subjects more representative, and results more generalizable. Presupposed is that the necessary first step, that of Definition, has in fact already been taken, that we know in theory who is and who is not a "homosexual" even if present social circumstances prevent us in practice from sorting real people into this and related categories.

This article argues to the contrary. Although each may himself or herself be certain about who merits inclusion within a category, the lack of consensus between workers brings into doubt the direct comparability of their results (cf. Creson, 1978; Hoffman, 1976).

Consider the following definitions of *homosexual*:

1. The English word homosexual, defined as a person who prefers the sexual company of persons of his or her own sex, corresponds to none of the Belém categories. (Fry, 1985, p. 142)
2. I do not diagnose patients as homosexual unless they have engaged in overt homosexual behavior. (I. Bieber, quoted in McIntosh, 1968, p. 182)

3. I would characterize the homosexual person . . . as one who is motivated in adult life by a definite preferential erotic attraction to members of the same sex and who usually (but not necessarily) engages in overt sexual relations with them. (Marmor, 1980, p. 5)
4. Clarification can be achieved if we conclude that there is no such *thing* as a *homosexual*. (Pattison, 1974, p. 341)

The first example requires a single criterion of psychological preference which only the actor can verify; opposing this emic standard, the second definition requires an etic, or outsider standard of observable behavior; the third definition straddles this emic/etic line. The last quote dismisses altogether the category as lacking a real world referent. Although they all report on "homosexuals," if each of these workers adheres to his defined universe when identifying subjects, their samples, and thereby the results, will not be comparable.

Riess (1980, pp. 300-301) notes a similar breadth afflicting *homosexuality*. Examples for this word include these three:

1. . . . from the psychobiological point of view . . . homosexuality = sexual behavior with a member of the organism's own sex. (Denniston, 1980, p. 26)
2. I have always been bothered by the definition of homosexuality as behavior. Scratching is a behavior. Homosexuality is a way of being, one that can completely influence a person's life and shape its meaning and direction. (Grahn, 1984, p. xiv)
3. In its generic sense the word homosexuality includes numerous activities and social transactions between persons of the same gender. The all-male board of directors, the businessman's club, the army, the girl's school, the religious order, the church women's circles are all "homosexuals" in this primary sense of the word. (Weltge, 1969, p. vii)

Again, the variance is striking. The first definition suggests a fairly strict behavioral criterion which is rejected by the second; the third so broadens the referent of the word as to render it conceptually useless.

This third definition introduces yet another difficulty. What is the relationship between *homosexual* and *homosexuality*? The ease with which Weltge shifts from one to the other suggests a synonymity, the words differing on syntactic rather than semantic properties. Counterexamples to such an equation, however, do exist. Whitam and Mathy (1986), for instance, after defining *homosexual* in emic terms of attraction (p. 2), later define *homosexuality* in etic terms of behavior (p. 32).

Another assumed synonym is *gay* (Ashley, 1979; Cory, 1965; Farrell, 1972; Niemoeller, 1965). If this relationship formerly held, it may no longer. Murray (1982, p. 7) reports the following from one of his informants:

> . . . there are others who have a lot of homosexual, um, "release" shall we say?–like they make it every day in some sordid tearoom, for instance, but would never admit to being gay. [What are they? What would you call them?] Closet cases. They're homosexual, but they aren't gay.

Divergence between *gay* and *homosexual* has been argued to be based on a preference for a chosen moniker over a medical label (Hodges & Hutter, [1974]). Allan Young (quoted by Hayes, 1976, p. 262) takes this separation one step further:

> . . . saying "I am gay" has the important element of self-definition to it. It is not the negative definition of others (homo, lezzie, queer, pansy, fruit) but a positive term we can call our own. . . . The term homosexual does not comply with the need of self-definition, because the term was given to us by doctors and other "scientists" who have not generally been our friends.

Through such associations, choice of words can be taken to indicate sociopolitical ideology (Stanley, 1974).

Lesbian has not been spared similar confusion, its range in many ways paralleling what we saw for *homosexuality*:

> In defining lesbianism we can offer four possible positions, in order of increasing breadth. First, lesbianism could be defined

in a strict way as genital sexuality between two people with female genitals. Secondly, we could define as lesbian any strong relationship between women with at least a *possibility* for such genital sex. . . . Thirdly, we could call lesbian any intense relationship or primary commitment between women that they subjectively experience as "love". . ., even if genital sexuality is not even a possibility. Finally, *any* affectional interaction between women . . . might be considered lesbian–one feminist has argued that since every daughter loves her mother, all women are lesbian. (Feinbloom, Fleming, Kijewski, & Schulter, 1976, p. 69)

If this quote builds from the narrow to the broad, it might also illustrate the progression from the useful to the meaningless. Similarly, without any guidelines or standards, Lockard's (1985, p. 84) statement that "a lesbian is anyone who says she is" cannot help but do more methodological harm than good.

A sociolinguistic description of how *homosexuality*, *homosexual*, and *gay* are used in "real life" follows, and focuses on issues of time, attitude, and style. Each presents its own problems for gay and lesbian studies. An attempt is made to use these results to establish definitional boundaries for each of these three critical terms. Linking the two projects is the philosophy that a purely theory-generated definition is in this case inferior to one based on the way the word is used by those most directly concerned, the men and women who live with these terms as labels (cf. Myrdal, 1962, p. lxxiv). For reasons explained below, no comparable quantitative data were gathered regarding *lesbian*; however, broad qualitative patterns are presented.

DESCRIPTION

Method

Issues of selected periodicals were examined, noting instances of the tokens *gay*, *homosexual*, and *homosexuality*. Each occurrence was placed into one of six use-type categories: Person-NOUN,

Activity-NOUN, and ADJectives modifying either Persons, Social Institutions, Behaviors, or Things. *Newsweek* and *Christianity Today* were selected to provide a contrast between attitudes toward homosexuality; while many of *Christianity Today*'s editorials may be characterized as negative (e.g., Kantzer, 1983), *Newsweek* provides indirect evidence of a comparatively more positive stance by its prominent featuring of gay individuals (e.g., Harvey Fierstein: Kroll, 1983), and in the extensive cover article devoted to the gay lifestyle (Reese & Abramson, 1986), attention unequalled by *Christianity Today*.

All articles from these periodicals listed on Infotrac under "Homosexuality" as of June 1986 are included, and constitute the NEW data set: *Newsweek* = 28 articles, *Christianity Today* = 18. The OLD set is an exhaustive listing of all entries in the *Reader's Guide to Periodical Literature* for the years 1965-1970: *Newsweek* = 8, *Christianity Today* = 8.

The Advocate and the *Journal of Homosexuality* were selected to examine the contrast between formal and informal writing styles. Two issues of each were selected haphazardly: *Advocate* issues 445 and 450, and *Journal* issues *12*(2) and *13*(1). Endnotes and bibliographies were excluded from *Journal* data; advertisements from *Advocate* data.

Results from this study are presented in Table 1. Scores are the percentage of *homosexual* tokens accrued in each use-type. Differences of ten percentage points or less are interpreted as being insignificant.

A second source of data is a questionnaire distributed during the 11th Annual Southeastern Conference for Lesbians and Gay Men held in New Orleans in June 1986. Respondents were asked to select, for each of 16 sentences, whether *gay* or *homosexual* seemed more appropriate to them. These sentences varied by style (informal/formal), attitude (positive/negative), and part-of-speech (noun/adjective). Respondents also wrote answers to several open questions. Only those respondents who rated themselves 5 or 6 (on a 0-6 scale) in terms of their "degree of homosexual orientation" are included. Omitting seventeen 1-4s, 99 questionnaires remained for statistical analyses.

Scoring was dichotomous, where "Gay" = 0 and "Homosexual" = 1. Deviation from the mean of possible scores for each variable indicates the degree of response preference. No sex differences were found.

Results

Changes due to time. This part considers whether vocabulary differences emerged between the pre-and post-Stonewall eras (cf. Schwanberg, 1985). Those changes which can be attributed to the passing of time–and, implicitly, to associated social changes–are minimally those which occur in both *Christianity Today* and *Newsweek.* Significant for us is that for no use-type in either title did *homosexual* see a meaningful increase from OLD to NEW. Any change was inevitably a decline, and can be accounted for by a rise in the popularity of alternative terms. Activity-NOUN is notable for its stable preference for *homosexual.*

Both periodicals in the NEW set significantly increased the frequency with which they refer to persons as "gays" rather than as "homosexuals." This change may be accounted for by the reasonableness that "a group should be able to determine its own name" (Dynes, 1985, p. vi), and that since Stonewall *gay* has become the appellation of choice.

Likewise, both now modify the majority of inanimate objects with *gay*, a change more difficult to explain. One possibility is that as gay subculture attained higher visibility, nouns not previously associated with the lifestyle appeared in this context: *beer, magazine*, and *curriculum*, for instance. Such nouns lacked a precedent of *homosexual* modification, and consequently may have been automatically modified by the new word referring by that time to the possessors of the artifact.

Since use of these terms has altered significantly over time, literature from opposite ends of a temporal span may not be directly comparable. Should *gay* and *homosexual* be determined not to be interchangeable, then older reports written when *homosexual* was the only word for subjects may need to be reexamined to ascertain which group was actually sampled.

Attitudinal differences. The similarities between two editorials separated by fifteen years ("The Bible and the Homosexual," 1968;

Table 1

Percent of homosexual tokens in six use-types

	CHRISTIANITY TODAY		NEWSWEEK		ADVOCATE	JOURNAL OF HOMOSEXUALITY
	OLD	NEW	OLD	NEW		
Person-NOUN	95%(60/3)	75%(95/32)	100%(69/0)	31%(55/122)	13%(11/71)	96%(245/11)
Activity-NOUN	99 (70/1)	99 (89/1)	100 (20/0)	89 (48/6)	87 (26/4)	99 (178/1)
Person-ADJ	56 (5/4)	55 (36/29)	75 (12/4)	15 (29/164)	3 (7/237)	45 (99/120)
Institution-ADJ	67 (24/12)	57 (39/29)	60 (15/10)	11 (14/115)	1 (2/157)	40 (36/53)
Behavior-ADJ	91 (21/2)	95 (81/4)	94 (16/1)	49 (11/12)	15 (7/40)	56 (40/31)
Thing-ADJ	60 (3/2)	33 (3/6)	40 (6/9)	6 (5/85)	0 (0/93)	50 (9/9)
Token Totals	88%(183/24)	77%(343/101)	85%(138/24)	24%(162/504)	8%(53/602)	73%(607/225)

Note: Percent of homosexual tokens (# homosexual tokens/# gay tokens)

34

Kantzer, 1983) establishes *Christianity Today*'s attitude toward homosexuality as both constant and negative. The data show that *Christianity Today* consistently prefers the use of *homosexual* in both OLD and NEW sets.

On the other hand, for all other categories besides Activity-NOUN, NEW *Newsweek* differs dramatically from *Christianity Today* in its word choices despite an initial similarity, and uses *homosexual* in the minority of cases. These data suggest that *Newsweek*'s increasingly positive attitude is paralleled by a change in language, just as the lack of attitude change by *Christianity Today* corresponds to a stability of language use. Attitude toward homosexuality, then can influence, if not determine word choice.

Results from the questionnaire support this association between attitude and token use. Statements expressing negative attitudes favored *homosexual* responses (Mean = 3.454, t = 3.069, p < .005), while positive sentences elicited *gay* (Mean = 0.899, t = 15.734, p < .0001). These strong statistical results are no doubt influenced by the respondents' full consciousness of the relationship, as illustrated by the following comments:

> I tend not to use the term *homosexual*. I see it as derogatory almost. I feel people who use *homosexual* are frequently uncomfortable with gays and gay lifestyle. [26 year old male]
>
> I never like to use the word *homosexual*, because it raises feelings related to antigay oppression; I use it when I need those overtones. [21 year old male]
>
> *Homosexual* has totally negative connotations for me because I first heard the label used by "moral" heterosexuals. [35 year old male]

Since negative attitudes demonstrably lead to the predominance of *homosexual*, these respondents display a tendency to infer from *homosexual* tokens a negative attitude. Excessive use of *homosexual*, then, may connote to others an archaic and perhaps negative attitude. Given this pattern of emotional reaction from members of the subject population, prudence suggests using *homosexual* sparingly in their presence. Otherwise the researcher risks inadvertently communicating a negative attitude toward the subject's lifestyle.

Stylistic differences. By examining word choice in *The Advocate* and the *Journal of Homosexuality*, this part considers whether formal (scholarly) publications will favor different vocabulary than do informal (mass) media.

Only in the Activity-NOUN use-type is *homosexual* the preferred word for the *Advocate*. In no other use-type does the percentage of *homosexual* tokens rise above 15%. The *Journal*, on the other hand, never falls below 40%, and the NOUN classes are especially high. Clearly, the *Journal* favors *homosexual* to the point of offering no alternatives for nouns.

The link between preference of *homosexual* and formal style is most likely historical. *Homosexual* was introduced earlier than *gay* (1869 as opposed to 1933: Herzer, 1985; Dynes, 1985; *homosexuality* was not introduced into the English language until 1897: Bardis, 1980). Moreover, *homosexual* was introduced in a scientific tract, while *gay* is attested in a dictionary of slang. From these facts alone one could predict the scientific, and hence the formal literature to favor *homosexual*.

Questionnaires yielded significant results only for informal style's preference for *gay* tokens (Mean = 1.8980; t = 10.805; p < .0001). Failure to validate a *homosexual*/formal relationship may have one of two explanations. First, the sentences may not have been sufficiently formal to elicit the expected reaction (#9: *Gay/Homosexual* leaders have been quick to endorse higher levels of funding for AIDS research). More likely is that judgments of formality are tied as much to the setting as to the statement. Contextless sentences may not signal the requisite formality levels. Conversely, the informal sentences are clearly just that (#14: He blames every bad thing that's ever happened to him on his *being gay/homosexuality*), allowing a significant relationship between this style and language to emerge.

Respondents themselves acknowledge that *gay* and *homosexual* vary stylistically:

I have problems with the term *gay* for scientific writing. In every other context I prefer *gay*. [37 year old female]
Homosexual is a good word to use in technical/legal instanc-

es, whereas, *gay* tends to be more appropriate under social circumstances. [29 year old male]

A conundrum for researchers is that the linguistic style of their professional medium converges with that of the gay community's antagonists (note the discussion on attitudinal differences). The academic preference for *homosexual* runs the risk that subjects will categorize the scientist in among their other opponents based on his or her pattern of language use, and react accordingly. Social scientists particularly may want to consider a more flexible style that accurately reflects the linguistic habits of their subjects. As June Reinisch of the Kinsey Institute comments, "If the research is not done in the vernacular,–in the words of the group–then it doesn't do any good" (Weiss, 1989). Further, when subjects report themselves to be gay and otherwise speak of things "gay," the researcher should report it as such, and not translate this term into the scientific *homosexual*.

DEFINITION

Having described how *homosexual, homosexuality,* and *gay* are used, we will now attempt to construct scientifically useful definitions. It is important to keep in mind what should and should not be expected of a definition. Its utility is to bring "together for our attention a number of phenomena which are in reality, and not merely in appearance, closely related to one another" (Radcliffe-Brown, 1952, p. 117). Its purpose is *not* to *explain* the phenomena represented therein. Criteria identifying individuals for inclusion within a category should never be confounded with post facto, statistical descriptions of the group, since such conclusions are generated by studying groups previously constructed by the definition.

The definition must also be as independent of theory as possible, since theory can change. Our perspective on the group will change, but our identification of the core phenomena should be as stable as possible; our understanding of the research focus can become more detailed, but that focus should not shift.

Identification is accomplished by enumerating criteria which distinguish category members. In an ideal situation, these criteria are necessary and sufficient. The "real" world, however, is better described by radial than by Aristotelian categories, and hence any proffered definition of a category prototype can fail to include easily some cases (Lakoff, 1987). In fact, Waismann (1960, p. 120) holds that this is *necessarily* the case for most empirical concepts, so that "it is not possible to define a concept . . . with absolute precision, i.e., in such a way that every nook and cranny is blocked against entry of doubt. That is what is meant by the open texture of a concept."

For instance, Murray (1984) argues that not all gays are homosexual, or Marmor (1980) that one need not engage in sexual activity to be homosexual. These may be ecologically valid qualifications, but they pertain to the periphery of the population prototype. Attempts to allow for exceptional cases within the prototype are largely responsible for the excessive relativism plaguing definitions, and thereby research in gay and lesbian studies. But as Bernard (1941, p. 507) points out, "the only area of sociological science in which we can standardize definition and reduce relativity to a veritable minimum is that of the hypothetical norm or ideal definition."

This section offers definitional limits to the key gay and lesbian studies terms *homosexuality, homosexual,* and *gay.* In keeping with Bernard's advice, they are idealized to increase utility. Although these definitions are designed to maximize inclusion, some cases will inevitably fall outside their scope, no matter how they are formed, due to the open texture of empirical concepts. The implication is not that these cases are irrelevant to gay and lesbian studies, but only that they are sufficiently exceptional not to warrant inclusion in the unmodified use of the key terms.

The previous section studied variables which influence the choice between *homosexual* and *gay.* All contexts favored the use of *homosexuality* in the Activity-NOUN use-type, and this is the only use-type which displays a universal consensus. The conservative approach, then, directs that this word be restricted to only this use. Upon this foundation can be built our first definition:

D1: *Homosexuality* refers *only* to overt sexual activity between actors of the same sex, and conveys no new information about psychological states or social meanings. Only with this stipulation can *homosexuality* be meaningfully applied to other animals besides humans (cf. Ford & Beach, 1951; Weinrich, 1976).

If *homosexuality* is strictly limited to activity (thus rejecting as an oxymoron "latent homosexuality"), the second definition follows uncontroversially:

> **D2**: *Homosexual* as an adjective should be restricted to overt acts and behaviors, particularly those either overtly sexual or intended to result in such (homosexual cruising, homosexual rape). It should be applied only to those psychological and social dimensions which pertain immediately to or otherwise motivate sexual behaviors (homosexual orientation, homosexual interest). Words which imply more than sexual activity (community, lifestyle, church) should not be modified by *homosexual*.

More difficult is specifying the referent for the noun *homosexual*. Almost everyone rejects that those who *do* homosexual acts *are* homosexual. Still, some individuals are meaningfully referred to as homosexuals, leaving to us the task of identifying the "indexical particulars" (Weinberg, 1978) which distinguish between a person performing homosexual acts and a homosexual.

Proponents of role theory point us in a useful direction when they argue that homosexual behavior and homosexual identity are not necessarily coincidental, and that "the homosexual should be seen as playing a social role rather than as having a condition" (McIntosh, 1968, p. 184). Membership within the category becomes contingent less upon the acts performed than upon the context in which these acts occur. Societies which lack homosexual roles are thereby said to also lack homosexuals, although not necessarily persons engaging in homosexuality.

The thrust of this theory is to attempt to explain the etiology of homosexuality, to argue against an essentialist interpretation and to offer in its stead a constructionist one (Richardson, 1983-84). As such we cannot use it directly in an atheoretical definition. Yet the notion of roles may still be taken up, indicative as it is of specialized knowledge and skills required to successfully accomplish the goal of the activity that is *homosexuality*:

> **D3**: *Homosexual* as a noun refers to persons practicing homosexuality who are also knowledgeable and proficient in the cultural or subcultural expectations of appropriate behaviors associated with homosexual activities. Examples of these might include cruising in styles acceptable and effective for various settings, and knowing where cruise spots are located. This word does not imply any etiological theory or psychological states (e.g., that the person has a particular kind of self-concept or identity); these extra meanings should be ascribed through adjectives (preferential homosexual, compulsive homosexual).

Excerpts from questionnaire respondents both ratify these definitions of *homosexual* and point the way toward distinguishing between it and *gay*:

> *Homosexual* defines a behavior; *gay* on the other hand defines an acceptance of the behavior, a mind set, by an individual. [23 year old male]
>
> I don't believe *gay* or *homosexual* are really related words. *Gay* describes a way of life. *Homosexual* may have nothing to do with *gay*. For example, many non-gay men (and women) do homosexual things, i.e., participate in homosexual acts. But there is nothing gay about those incidents. [24 year old male]

Representatives of the academic community echo these sentiments. For instance, Williams (1986, p. 223) observes that

> elderly Indians generally preferred to use the word "gay" rather than "homosexual." They see the latter as focusing on sexual behavior, whereas their focus is on a person's character. "Gay," with its connotation of life-style beyond sexual behavior seems to fit in more closely with an Indian understanding.

Gay, then, identifies the person who not only engages in homosexuality, and is homosexual, but also has a particular attitude or mindset about this activity. This attitude is typically described as positive and integrating, expanding into broader social concerns and relationships beyond the merely sexual. We thereby arrive at two last definitions:

> **D4**: *Gay* as a noun refers to homosexuals who share social and psychological attributes such as positive self-identity (as far as their sexual orientation is concerned); studies to more fully explicate these attributes are needed; and
>
> **D5**: *Gay* as an adjective should modify only such nouns as are consistent with the future explicated psychological and socially-oriented qualities. Predominant use is expected with social institutions and objects which imply the existence of such institutions.

CONCLUSIONS

A review of the literature demonstrated a fundamental inconsistency in the way workers define key gay and lesbian studies terms. Individual students construct their own definitions based on either general theory or particular research needs. The contribution of this study is to offer a set of five definitions which both conform to the nature of definitions *per se* and derive from empirical data about actual language use.

Changes over time, the speaker's attitude, and the style of the communication medium all were shown to influence word choice. Each carries its own set of problems regarding the practice of a maturing and collaborative gay and lesbian studies. These data also support a persistent identification of *homosexuality* as an activity, suggesting that the word be restricted to this meaning. The offered definitions for *homosexual* and *gay* as noun and adjective are largely the logical consequences of this initial equation.

It is our belief that these definitions will prove to be of maximum utility to gay and lesbian studies because they are (1) ecologically valid, and ensure that researchers and the researched are not talking past one another; (2) theoretically noncommittal, and can serve to identify the phenomena of interest regardless of the intellectual posture from which they are to be scrutinized; and (3) methodologically helpful, in that they provide few but clear criteria for subject selection.

As suggested throughout, the problem of definition is not a theoretical nicety, but rather has the most profound impact on a science because it is used to identify subjects for research. This paper concludes, then, with some suggestions about how these definitions would influence this phase of methodology.

Workers will continue to draw their subjects from the same sources. What should change, though, is the assumption that gays and homosexuals identify the same population, when in fact the first is but a subset of the second. More research is needed to articulate exactly how they are differentiated, but the definitions here may indicate some likely dimensions. In any event, the subject's own language should serve as a cue as to which group he or she belongs.

Self-reports regarding acts of homosexuality, or the role proficiency requirements of the homosexual are not necessarily true, and sometimes caution may need to be exercised about accepting such claims on their face. Less caution need be exercised in applying the label to persons who are known to meet the proficiency requirements but who do not consider themselves to be homosexual; *homosexual* describes an informed pattern of activity–as opposed to *homosexuality*, which references the sexual activity alone–and not an identity. *Gay*, on the other hand, is an identity shared by a subset of (perhaps mostly Western) homosexuals, without describing any additional sexual behaviors. Thus, no one can be meaningfully called "gay" if the subject rejects the label.

If *gay* identifies one subset of the homosexual universe, then other terms or phrases will be needed to refer to other, non-gay subsets. Again, more work will be needed to specify the relevant differentiating dimensions. For instance, if a major motivation for gays to engage in homosexuality is the emic quality of attraction toward the same sex, another subset of the homosexual population might usefully be defined by its motivating quality of "fear" of the opposite sex (cf. Marmor, 1988). Still another example of a non-gay homosexual might be a practitioner of "ritualized homosexuality" as discussed by Herdt (1984). As these distinctions are made, the use of words like *gay* and *homosexual* must become self-conscious rather than an ill-considered reflex.

Just as *gay* is argued to be but one segment of the *homosexual* universe, at the time of project design *lesbian* was assumed to be semantically subordinate to *gay*, being the female equivalent to *gay man*. This project was not intended to delve into vocabulary embedded so far as this, and hence there are no data regarding *lesbian* comparable to those offered in Table 1.

Yet one of the open questions did probe into the issue of the meaning of *lesbian* for all respondents and, for women, the more general issue of self-referral. Responses indicate that the aforementioned assumption may have been unfounded. It certainly is representative of the "male" attitude towards *lesbian*:

> [I use *lesbian*] when referring to a gay woman. To me *gay* refers to all people (male & female) with same-sex preferences. [29 year old male]

Significantly, most males in this sample seem to use *lesbian* out of conscious acquiescence to women's choice, not because they themselves agree with the word use:

> I use *lesbian* only when women friends insist that I do—we are all "gay" people. [32 year old male]
>
> I use the word *lesbian* out of deference to my gay sisters. . . . [46 year old male]

More important here, though, is how women view the term. Surprisingly, at the time the data were gathered, *lesbian* was not universally favored:

> I hate the word *lesbian*, & avoid using it to refer to myself or to other women. I use *gay*. [28 year old female]
>
> [I use *lesbian*] only when it seems "politically correct"

around other lesbians. I really rarely use lesbian to describe myself. I usually say I'm gay. [29 year old female]

Impressionistically, *lesbian* does seem to have gained in overall popularity since 1986. And while males seemed passive on the matter ("The only reason I use [*lesbian*] is to respect my sisters. I wonder if they like it?"), females foreshadowed the actual path taken in the last five years:

I say that I am gay, as that was the first word I learned after *queer*, back in 1951. If I were speaking to a group of younger gay women, I would say "lesbian," as that is more comfortable for most of them. They relate to the word *gay* as meaning men. [55 year old female]

Indeed, *gay* does seem to have acquired a gender marking of + male. This has produced significant language changes, some of which are being played out in the pages of *The Advocate*. Beginning in October, 1990, the banner was changed to advertise the periodical as the "national gay *and lesbian* newsmagazine" (Rouilard, 1990). This explicit inclusion by the community's flagship periodical perhaps marks the demise of *gay* as a nongender-marked term.

The vocal reaction from some–uniformly male–quarters has been unfavorable. Wrote one reader:

It has been my feeling for some time that lesbians should be charged with separatism. They insist that they be called lesbian. I have yet to figure out why they can't be included in a sexually nonspecific label. Are they so insecure that they can't share the umbrella of *gay* or *homosexual*? (Abernathy, 1990)

In fact, a new word has emerged to fulfill the function once performed by *gay*, that of including both males and females: *queer*. This word can be attested as having precisely this meaning by design (Heller, 1990) and by inference (Elton, 1990). Use of this word has also met with mixed reactions, largely due to its past negative connotations, and present politically radical ones. Still, it may eventually fill the void left by the semantic drift of *gay*.

REFERENCES

Abernathy, J.B. (1990, November 6). Letter: New but not improved? *The Advocate*, p. 11.

Ashley, L.R.N. (1979). Kinks and queens. *Maledicta, 3*(1/2), 215-256.

Bardis, P.D. (1980). A glossary of homosexuality. *Maledicta, 4*(1), 59-63.

Bell, A.P., & Weinberg, M.S. (1978). *Homosexualities.* New York: Simon & Schuster.

Bernard, L.L. (1941). The definition of definition. *Social Forces, 19*(4), 500-510.

"The Bible and the Homosexual." (1968). *Christianity Today, 12*(8), 24-25.

Chambliss, D.J., & Dunlap, W.P. (1977). *Experimental design and analysis.* New Orleans: Tulane University.

Cory, D.W. (1965). The language of the homosexual. *Sexology, 32*(3), 163-165.

Creson, D.L. (1978). Homosexuality. *Encyclopedia of Bioethics*, vol. 2 (pp. 667-671). New York: Free Press.

Denniston, R.H. (1980). Ambisexuality in animals. In J. Marmor (Ed.), *Homosexual behavior: A modern reappraisal* (pp. 25-40). New York: Basic Books.

Dynes, W. (1985). *Homolexis.* New York: Gay Academic Union.

Elton, L. (1990, October 23). A word to the wise [Letter to the editor]. *The Advocate*, p. 11.

Farrell, R.A. (1972). The argot of the homosexual subculture. *Anthropological Linguistics, 14*(3), 97-109.

Feinbloom, D.H., Fleming, M., Kijewski, V., & Schulter, M.P. (1976). Lesbian/feminist orientation among male-to-female transsexuals. *Journal of Homosexuality, 2*(1), 59-71.

Ford, C., & Beach, F.A. (1951). *Patterns of sexual behavior.* New York: Harper.

Fry, P. (1985). Male homosexuality and spirit possession in Brazil. *Journal of Homosexuality, 11*(3/4), 137-153.

Gonsiorek, J.C. (1982). Mental health: Introduction. In W. Paul, J.D. Weinrich, J.C. Gonsiorek, & M.E. Hotvedt (Eds.), *Homosexuality: Social, psychological, and biological issues* (pp. 57-70). Beverly Hills: Sage.

Gorsky, D.P. (1981). *Definition.* (Translated by Sergei Syrovatkin.) Moscow: Progress Publishers.

Grahn, J. (1984). *Another mother tongue.* Boston: Beacon Press.

Hayes, J.J. (1976). Gayspeak. *Quarterly Journal of Speech, 62*, 256-266.

Heller, S. (1990, October 24). Gay- and lesbian-studies movement gains acceptance in many areas of scholarship and teaching. *The Chronicle of Higher Education*, A4+.

Herdt, G.H. (1984). Ritualized homosexual behavior in the male cults of Melanesia, 1862-1983. In G. Herdt (Ed.), *Ritualized homosexuality in Melanesia* (pp. 1-81). Berkeley: University of California Press.

Herzer, M. (1985). Kentbeny and the nameless love. *Journal of Homosexuality, 12*(1), 1-26.

Hodges, A., & Hutter, D. (1974). *With downcast gays*. [pamphlet]. Pomegranate Press.

Hoffman, M. (1976). Homosexuality. In F.A. Beach (Ed.), *Human sexuality in four perspectives* (pp. 164-189). Baltimore: Johns Hopkins University Press.

Kantzer, K.S. (1983). Homosexuals in the church. *Christianity Today, 27*(8), 8.

Kroll, J. (1983, June 20). His heart is young and gay. *Newsweek*, p. 71.

Lakoff, G. (1987). *Women, fire, and dangerous things*. Chicago: University of Chicago Press.

Lockard, D. (1985). The lesbian community: An anthropological approach. *Journal of Homosexuality, 11*(3/4), 83-95.

McIntosh, M. (1968). The homosexual role. *Social Problems, 16*(2), 182-192.

Marmor, J. (1980). Overview: The multiple roots of homosexual behavior. In J. Marmor (Ed.), *Homosexual behavior: A modern reappraisal* (pp. 3-22). New York: Basic Books.

Marmor, J. (1988). Homosexuality. *Encyclopedia Americana*, Vol. 14 (pp. 333-335).

Murray, S.O. (1982). A folk theory of homosexual categorization: Extract from an interview. *Anthropological Research Group on Homosexuality Newsletter, 4*(1/2), 6-7.

Murray, S.O. (1984). *Social theory, homosexual realities* [Gai Saber Monograph No. 3.]. New York: Gay Academic Union.

Myrdal, G. (1962). *An American dilemma* (20th Anniversary Edition). New York: Harper & Row.

Niemoeller, A.F. (1965). A glossary of homosexual slang. *Fact, 2*, 25-27.

Pattison, E.M. (1974). Confusing concepts about the concept of homosexuality. *Psychiatry, 37*, 340-349.

Radcliffe-Brown, A.R. (1952). *Structure and function in primitive society*. New York: Free Press.

Reese, M., & Abramson, P. (1986, January 13). One family's struggle. *Newsweek*, p. 55-58.

Richardson, D.L. (1983-84). The dilemma of essentiality in homosexuality. *Journal of Homosexuality, 9*(2/3), 79-90.

Riess, B.F. (1980). Psychological tests in homosexuality. In J. Marmor (Ed.), *Homosexual behavior: A modern reappraisal* (pp. 296-311). New York: Basic Books.

Rouilard, R. (1990, October 9). Comment: To be gay in this decade, one must also be lesbian. *The Advocate*, p. 6.

Schwanberg, S.L. (1985). Changes in labeling homosexuality in health sciences literature: A preliminary investigation. *Journal of Homosexuality, 12*(1), 51-73.

Stanley, J. (1974). When we say "Out of the closets." *College English, 36*(3), 385-391.

Stoller, R.J. (1980). Problems with the term "homosexuality." *Hillside Journal of Clinical Psychiatry, 2*(1), 3-25.

Waismann, F. (1960). Verifiability. In A. Flew (Ed.), *Essays on logic and language, First series* (pp. 117-144). Oxford: Basil Blackwell.

Weinberg, T.S. (1978). On "doing" and "being" gay. *Journal of Homosexuality*, 4(2), 143-156.

Weinrich, J.D. (1976). *Human reproductive strategy*. Unpublished Ph.D. dissertation. Cambridge: Harvard University.

Weiss, R. (1989, July 8). Desperately seeking sexual statistics. *Science News*, *136*(2), 28.

Weltge, R.W. (Ed.). (1969). *The same sex: An appraisal of homosexuality*. Philadelphia: Pilgrim Press.

Whitam, F.L., & Mathy, R.M. (1986). *Male homosexuality in four societies*. New York: Praeger.

Williams, W.L. (1986). *The spirit and the flesh: Sexual diversity in American Indian culture*. Boston: Beacon Press.

Deconstruction, Lesbian and Gay Studies, and Interdisciplinary Work: Theoretical, Political, and Institutional Strategies

ki namaste, PhD (cand.)

l'université du Québec à Montréal

SUMMARY. The problematic of cultural self-representation is examined in light of the development of lesbian and gay studies. The issues are examined through the lens of deconstruction as theoretical and political strategy. This examination suggests the value of interventionist work, and seeks to articulate an understanding of interdisciplinary work as exemplary of such an interventionist practice and politic. Relevant theoretical and political implications are explored, most especially in terms of the future developments of lesbian and gay studies.

More and more as we enter into the 1990s, lesbians and gay men are at the forefront in movements for social change, both within and outside of the academy. Our concerns can no longer be dismissed as "private issues," precisely because we have employed feminist

ki namaste is a doctoral student in semiotics at UQAM, l'université du Québec à Montréal. He has completed a great deal of research on the semiotics of safe sex advertisements, and is primarily interested in the regulation of difference within lesbian and gay male communities. His work focusses on the cultural resistance offered to this regulation of difference, most especially around questions of gender, identity, and sexuality. Correspondence may be addressed to: doctorat en sémiologie, a/s département d'études littéraires, UQAM, C.P. 8888, Succursale A, Montréal, Québec, H3C 3P8 Canada.

theory and practice to turn the public/private dualism on its head and render it permanently problematic. Within the academy, we have been demanding that our lives, our experiences, and our multitude ways of making sense of social meanings be researched. We have claimed that these ways of making sense of social relations are valid not only because they reflect our experience, but also because they expose the ways in which heterosexual hegemony regulates meanings so that they appear ordered, coherent, and unified. As we continue this work, and as we continue to engage in our research in the context of recent developments in feminist theory around issues of identity, difference, and representation, something else is happening within the institutional setting where we produce and present these thoughts.

Our concerns, our theoretical insights, our practical politics are no longer being ignored. I am not quite sure as to whether or not they are being taken seriously, but at any rate they are no longer being overlooked. As lesbians and gay men, we are being inserted (and are inserting ourselves) into the academy in ways heretofore unimaginable. It is not uncommon for us to present openly lesbian and gay material at conferences, and it is becoming more and more common for us to receive invitations to present our work. Yet where do these requests come from? Who is requesting our presence, and why do they want us there? Are they really willing to listen to what we have to say? And, perhaps most importantly, are they committed to acting on the structures of the academy which position us as Other in our daily lives? How do all of these questions relate to the development of lesbian and gay studies?

These are some of the questions I wish to consider in this article, particularly in light of deconstructionist theory and practice. I want to begin to consider some of the very practical, political, and theoretical options ''we'' as lesbians and gay men are faced with when we receive invitations to present at conferences, or to publish our work. Most particularly, I am interested in theorizing these issues in light of deconstruction–suggesting some of the political and theoretical lessons deconstruction (as a way of understanding the world, politics, and theory) has highlighted. With these lessons in mind, I seek to offer some tentative suggestions of future directions for lesbian and gay studies. My aim in so doing is not so much to develop a program of study as much as it is to suggest strategies of intervention.

More and more frequently, lesbians and gay men are being invited to speak at conferences, to participate in workshops, and to present at panels in order to provide "the (essential) lesbian/gay perspective." As individuals and communities who may be involved in such work, I think we need to understand the implications underlying such a request, as well as what we can do if/when we receive one. Requesting a gay/lesbian perspective for a conference or panel suggests that all lesbians and gay men have similar positions on issues, and obscures issues of difference and contradiction within lesbian and gay male communities and identities. Particularly given who as lesbians and gay men is situated within the academy, and given these peoples' positions of privilege vis-à-vis gender, race, class, ability, language, and region, white anglophone middle class lesbians and (more frequently) gay men are asked to not only represent, but be representative of all lesbians and gay men. The violence inherent within such a request is evident: lesbian and gay male self-representation distorts who, in fact, lesbians and gay men are, the varied and contradictory positions in which we are situated, and the myriad of ways we have of making sense of social meanings. Jeffrey Escoffier (1990) recounts an instance at the 1989 Yale Lesbian and Gay Studies conference, where discussion took place around the institutionalization of lesbian and gay studies. Careful analysis revealed that many of the courses taught in lesbian and gay studies have met with resistance. Escoffier (1990) analyzes the situation at Yale in which Wayne Kostenbaum discussed these issues:

> Some senior colleagues in his department had not wanted him to teach a course on homosexuality in literature. They eventually relented, but had insisted that he include "major" writers. Kostenbaum's dilemma–the course covered a period when he thought there were few if any major writers who were women or people of color–exemplifies the need for awareness and thoughtfulness on the issues of race and gender. (p. 48)

Similarly, after submitting a proposal for a presentation on the concepualizations of body fluids within safe sex advertisements, I was invited to speak on a cultural studies panel. What I found most intriguing was that I was to present at a session entitled "Semiotics and Sociology of Gender," even though my abstract was not centrally concerned with issues of gender. When introduced at the session, the chair said that I was to address the representation of the gay subject within safe sex advertisements. Several things struck me: firstly, that I was one of three anglophone white men who were to present on the "semiotics of gender"; secondly, that the chair of the session who was responsible for the selection of the presentations, made an unequivocal equation between sex, gender, and sexuality; thirdly, the assumption that gay subjectivity was so monolithic we could speak about it in its singular and uncomplicated form; and finally, that I was selected to present (in part) not because of the theoretical concerns I was raising in my paper, but because of who I was perceived to be. Curiously, the absence of any women presenters was excused by my presence, and the assumption that a gay man would articulate a feminist position was prevalent. In this thinking, my presence was understood to serve the dual tokenist function of including both feminist and lesbian/gay perspectives.

To begin addressing issues of diversity, then, we who are involved in such (self) representation need to contextualize ourselves and our work. That is, we need to point out the fact that we are not representative of all lesbians and gay men, and that fags and dykes come from and out of everywhere. We need to explore the various contradictory subject-positions we inhabit, only some of which will be apparent based on the assumptions made upon hearing, seeing, and reading our work. And of course, we need to research the diversity within our communities, and to do this research on its own terms.

More than researching our subject-positions, however, we need to theorize how we come to occupy or resist various subject-positions within the academy, and what the operations of power are that lie behind (and within) these inscriptions. As Gayatri Spivak (1990a) argues, within the academy the center is al(l)ways defined in relation to the margins. She is frequently asked to represent the position of "Third World women," and notes:

> I find the demand on me to be marginal amusing. And as I
> have said, I'm tired of dining out on being an exile because

that has a long tradition and it is not one I want to identify myself with. But the question is a more complex one. In a certain sense, I think that there is nothing that is central. The centre is always constituted in terms of its own marginality. However, having said that, in terms of the hegemonic historical narrative, certain peoples have always been asked to cathect the margins so others can be defined as central. Negotiating between these two structures, sometimes I have to see myself as marginal in the eyes of others. (p. 40-41)

Spivak continues in arguing for the necessity of presenting oneself at the center even as the center doesn't exist. She calls for a strategic use of identity in order to both resist dominant epistemological and ontological assumptions about marginality, and in order to understand the operations of power which underlie notions of marginality and identity. A strategic adoption of a queer identity is also useful as a means of contesting (and surviving) heterosexism and homophobia within the academy.

Yet the dilemma we are faced with is one not unfamiliar to any minorities involved in self-representation. How do we employ identity strategically, and simultaneously avoid resubstantializing our positions of otherness? How are we able to politick for "positive images" and inclusion in course material without essentializing who "we" are? How do we engage in theoretical and political work within the academy which understands the structural, epistemological, and political reasons why "we" have been excluded for so long? And who do "we" mean by "we," anyway? I wish to explore these questions through the lens of deconstruction as theoretical and political strategy. I hope to outline some of the important issues which (various reading of) deconstruction have highlighted. Moreover, I wish to understand these recent theoretical developments in terms of their import for the political uses of marginalized individuals and communities within the academy.

DECONSTRUCTIONIST STRATEGY AND PRACTICE

In articulating an understanding of deconstructionist strategy and practice, I seek to offer alternative readings of several theoretical and political problems associated with deconstruction. Firstly, insofar as an orthodox reading of deconstruction privileges the text and intertextuality (Derrida's famous quotation that "there is nothing outside of the text"), subjectivity is theorized as entirely passive. Subject-formation and subject-position in such a reading occur only in relation to text, and the possibility of an agency of resistance is foreclosed. Secondly, in that deconstruction holds as one of its basic tenets the continual deferral of meaning and the interruption of any sort of easy closure in reading, it can never found a political programme in itself. That is, if any deconstructionist reading which situates the binary oppositions and the operations of power which underlie a text can be further deconstructed itself, then the possibility of any political reading is subverted. Deconstruction as a programme in itself by definition is rendered apolitical and depoliticized. It needs, therefore, to remain ever strategic and always-already in question. In this sense, then, it is useful to speak not of deconstruction as some monolithic enterprise, but rather to speak of deconstructionist strategies, readings, practices, and interventions. Finally, in North America at least, "deconstruction" has become one of those academic buzzwords like "subjectivity" and "postmodern" which can mean just about anything we may want it to! Not only are we capable of deconstructing the text, but we can also deconstruct the primitive, deconstruct the colonizer, deconstruct the subject, deconstruct the postmodern, and even deconstruct the deconstructor! What this use of the term "deconstruct" implies, however, is that deconstruction exists as a formula, and that it is centrally concerned with questions of exposing error. As Vincent Leitch (1983) notes,

> There is a worry that deconstruction is becoming predictable and rigid–that it is now a *method*. The recipe for Derridean deconstruction is: take any traditional concept or established formulation, invert its set of hierarchical terms, and subject them to fragmentation via an insistent principle of difference. After unhinging the elements in any structure or textual system toward radical free play, stand back and sift the rubble for hidden or unexpected formations. Tout these special findings as outlawed truths. (Hence the infamous *supplement* of the

Grammatology.) Mix all of this work with dashes of erotic lyricism and with apocalyptic intimations. Packaged within this quick codification–this easy parody–lies a rigid formulation of deconstruction as well as an anxious realization of the present crisis of deconstruction. No longer busy being born, deconstruction is busy dying. Or so it may now seem. (p. 262)

Rather than understanding deconstruction as a formula for exposing error, it is more productive and politically useful to employ it as a strategy in understanding the production of truths. As Derrida argues (quoted in Leitch, 1983), the issue of concern is that

It is clear it [difference] cannot be *exposed*. We can only expose what, at a certain moment, can become *present*, manifest; what can be shown, presented as present, a being–present in its truth, the truth of a present or the presence of a present. (p. 42)

Now that I have outlined some of the readings of deconstruction that I do not wish to offer (or reinforce), I need to articulate some of the common issues within deconstructionist practices, and their political import for the question I am concerned with at this time. Deconstruction teaches us that everything happens from within, that there is no "outside," and that it's important we not assume we could possibly be "outside." In situating ourselves as fags and dykes, we need to position ourselves as–whatever else–inside the academy and inside lesbian and gay male communities. Our work, then, and our strategic employment of identities, needs to reflect and utilize these positions.

Related, in that we are always-already inside, the concept of "border" is one which needs to be understood as part of a project which seeks to offer singular readings as self-present truths. The construction, regulation, and surveillance of such borders serves to establish closed readings, to produce truths and essentialize being-presence, and to invoke a unified (and passive) subject. Deconstructionist interventions allow us to understand the ways in which these boundaries are established, and how they obliterate difference and multiple (mis)readings in the name of the Same. These strategies seek to understand the binary oppositions which underline such divisions, as well as the ways in which they present themselves as foundational truths within epistemological and ontological statements.

A crucial question in a deconstructionist enterprise focussed on issues of identity and self-representation is: "What are we in the process of becoming?" Such a question revolves around the positioning of subjectivity, and not, in fact, around ontological presuppositions. Instead of focussing on who we are, thereby claiming who has the right to speak and represent, it investigates the history of how people are silenced, and what their responses to such silencing have been. Throughout, it remains critical of political and theoretical endeavours which resubstantialize the foundationalist categories of being we seek to resist, critique, and transform. And it remains committed to a politics of intervention, strategies which seek to open up meanings and disseminations, and readings which theorize a politics of agency, resistance, and transformation.

Spivak (1988) provides a useful summary of central issues and questions within deconstructive strategies:

> (T)he recognition, within deconstructive practice, of provisional and intractable starting points in any investigative effort; its disclosure of complicities where a will to knowledge would create oppositions; its insistence that in disclosing complicities the critic-as-subject is herself complicit with the object of her critique; its emphasis on "history" and upon the ethico-political as the "trace" of that complicity–the proof that we do not inhabit a clearly-defined critical space free of such traces; and, finally, the acknowledgement that its own discourse can never be adequate to its example. (p. 180)

There is much to use strategically within a deconstructionist practice in the political and theoretical interests of fags and dykes within the academy. Such a practice understands the assumptions (epistemological, ontological, theoretical) behind marginality, their presence in the cases of inviting a gay/lesbian presence at conferences, and their role in further substantializing positions of otherness. Deconstruction, as theoretical and political strategy, allows fags and dykes not only to understand how we have come to be–and remain–marginal within the academy, but also how we can situate ourselves so as to create our own meanings and articulate our own positions. Rather than assuming–whether ideally or naive-ly–that we are entirely outside, entirely Other, deconstructionist interventions are concerned with questions of negotiation. As such, the question at hand is how to negotiate with the structures of vio-lence which (re)produce alterity, rather than *who* is constituted by those structures. The question of "who" thus becomes reformulated in terms of how people are constituted, and relatedly, how these positions (or other ones) can be employed as/in resistance.

If we want to think about contesting, much less surviving, hetero-sexism in the academy, we need to consider how we have histori-cally been marginalized (ignored) as well as how we are presently being marginalized (tokenism). Moreover, we need to think about appropriate ways for us to negotiate with the structures which mar-ginalize us. As Spivak (1988) suggests, since the only subject who exists is always-already centered, the most theoretically and politi-cally "correct" strategy is to present oneself at the center. A strate-gic adoption of queer identity is useful in this regard, for it recog-nizes the impossibility of being a non-essentialist, and seeks to move beyond a limited analysis whereby only ontological issues are raised. In an effort to understand the epistemological, structural, and institutional constitution and positioning of subjects, a deconstruc-tionist enterprise understands "ontology" as contingent upon a myriad of practices of signification and epistemology within the contexts of a multitude of discursive frameworks.

The issue is not so much lesbians and gay men as *objects* of study, as it is our various subject-positions, how we come to occupy and/or resist them, and what the operations of power are which underline them. Research on these issues–our subject-positions–is both theoretically and politically fruitful (no pun intended), because it allows us to speak of ourselves on our own terms. Specifically, it engages our communities and identities, our experiences, our ways of making sense of social relations. And it permits us an analysis of not only our positions within the academy (and else-where/everywhere), but also of the ways in which the institutional operations of the academy organize knowledge so as to produce and reproduce alterity.

In order to negotiate the structures of violence which produce alterity within the academy, we are confronted with a challenge which requires more than a mere *insertion* of lesbians and gay men into existing curricula and programmes. Indeed, to simply call for more investigative efforts into lesbian and gay issues is to acritically reproduce the discursive structures in the academy which have been (and are) in part responsible for relegating us to the margins. Challenging these structures involves more than a simplistic "add fags and dykes and stir" remedy. It involves understanding the way knowledge is organized within the structure of the academy, and how such a framework by definition fragments our understandings, compartmentalizes issues, and contributes to a project which requires that the center be defined in relation to the margins.

DIRECTIONS FOR THE FUTURE: CHALLENGING DISCIPLINARY BOUNDARIES

In terms of strategies for displacing this epistemic violence, we need to engage in work which challenges disciplinary boundaries and the current epistemological and ontological limits set within them. To engage in interdisciplinary work is a practice which seeks to recognize and transform the current (un)reality of disciplinary boundaries. It understands the ways in which knowledge is currently carved up within academe, yet seeks to deconstruct the production of truths, the operations of power, and the assumptions about knowledge which are implicit in that apparatus. It implicitly–and sometimes explicitly–asks "Who's doing the carving?" and "In whose interest?" More than being concerned with questions of *who*, however, such endeavours focus on the production of alterity within disciplinary boundaries, seeking to undermine their authority and presence. In this context, interdisciplinary work can be understood as a politics of intervention, and as theoretically and politically necessary.

The development of interdisciplinary lesbian and gay studies could possibly mean a radically different understanding of the lives, experiences, and realities of lesbians and gay men. Perhaps most radically, it has the potential to even mean the complete and utter abandonment of "lesbian" and "gay" as labels used to signify ontological essence. As interdisciplinary work challenges the ways in which knowledge is carved up into neat little packages, packages which flatten the complexity and diversity of issues, it also understands the reasons which underlie an adoption of a lesbian/gay identity in the context of the institution of the university. That is, insofar as the institutionalization of disciplinary endeavours has meant that only certain questions get asked, only certain people studied, only certain issues raised, lesbians and gay men, along with feminists, People of Color, and many other marginalized groups and individuals have resisted such a limited understanding of the issues. One of the primary means of such resistance has been the strategic adoption of identity, and a concomitant employment of language which refers to the everyday lives and realities of people within specific historical, cultural, and discursive settings. To make sense of these events and issues, then, it is useful to employ the terms "lesbian" and "gay" provisionally. That is, these words refer not so much to some vague notion of ontological essence as much as they emphasize the underlying institutional structures which require that marginalized issues and people name themselves and demand attention. Of course, the adoption of lesbian/gay identities occurs outside of the institution of the university as well; the point I wish to make, however, is that historically it has only been with the adoption of these identities and the use of these terms that the academy has even admitted that these issues (these people) merit our scholarly attention. What I am suggesting further is that these identities and linguistic usages need to be contextualized in order that as marginalized groups and individuals, we not empower the very institutional and epistemological apparati which have silenced and ignored us for so long.

In keeping with a focus on the production of truths and a politics of intervention, such work could tread the delicate line between understanding the historic adoption of lesbian/gay identities, and refusing to be contained by these same words and frames of reference. That is, one of the greatest challenges facing lesbian and gay studies today is how to address the issues without essentializing who, in fact, one is talking about. In the 1990s, this is becoming increasingly complex. Indeed, it is no longer adequate to speak simply of "lesbians and gay men" and to refer to people who have sex exclusively with members of the same sex, or to refer to people as the "opposite" of heterosexuals. In the 1990s, more and more lesbians and gay men are public about the fact that they maintain a lesbian/gay identity, yet may at times have sex with members of another sex. Again, this is really nothing new; it's just OK to talk about it now–sort of. As Scott Tucker (1990) writes:

> Elsewhere, charming surprises occur. It's an open secret, for example, that men and women active in ACT UP (AIDS Coalition To Unleash Power) and Queer Nation are having sex together in unpredictable patterns, and with little sexual disorientation. Most are contentedly lesbian and gay, some are bisexual, a few are straight. This is possible in a time and milieu where they are able to achieve a strong community of resistance; within it, they take much for granted and don't feel their integrity is eroded when centers of sexual gravity shift for the duration of an affair or a night. Splendid: this is hedonism with a conscience, and one practical prefiguration of utopia. (p. 33)

Lesbian and gay studies needs to be able to theorize these sorts of issues as an integral aspect of lesbian/gay lives, experiences, and realities. The terms "lesbian" and "gay" can be understood thus as contingent on specific historic and institutional settings. It seems ironic that the future development of lesbian and gay studies may indeed suggest that lesbian/gay studies as such lends itself more appropriately to historical work. Yet it is also an exciting prospect, for it suggests that intervention is occurring everywhere–in our epistemologies, in our identities, in our sex lives.

Insofar as deconstruction is engaged in "provisional and intractable starting points," and insofar as interdisciplinary work seeks to understand the complexity of such positions, it would seem that it is aptly suited to the research task at hand. Yet what, precisely, does interdisciplinary work consist of? How are we to develop an analytic perspective without relying acritically on everything we have been taught that constitutes proper "knowledge" in our respective disciplines? And how do we go about teaching a politics of intervention and interdisciplinary work while we are simultaneously situated within disciplinary structures? Interdisciplinary work involves a constant interruption of accented theories and methods in order to question not only the uses to which they are put, but also the presuppositions and assumptions about knowledge which underlie them. As Stuart Hall (1990) argues, the development of cultural studies in the 1960s and 1970s involved understanding the ideological operations present within disciplinary practices, and situating these insights in terms of their regulative and normative functions. Hall (1990) writes:

> What we discovered was that serious interdisciplinary work does not mean that one puts up the interdisciplinary flag and then has a kind of coalition of colleagues from different departments, each of whom brings his or her own specialization to a kind of academic smorgasbord from which students can sample each of these riches in turn. Serious interdisciplinary work involves the intellectual risk of saying to professional sociologists that what they say sociology is, is not what it is. We had to teach what we thought a kind of sociology that would be of service to people studying culture would be, something we could not get from self-designated sociologists. It was never a question of which disciplines would contribute to the development of this field, but of how one could decenter or destabilize a series of interdisciplinary fields. We had to respect and engage with the paradigms and traditions of knowledge and of empirical and concrete work in each of these disciplinary areas in order to construct what we called cultural studies or cultural theory. (p. 16)

Interdisciplinary work, then, is not a mere addition of various disciplinary approaches. It cuts within and across these fields, interrupting its own project in the sense that it subverts any sort of easy closure. Remaining forever strategic, it lays claim to the political value of interventionist work, and requires that we understand the epistemic violence inherent within disciplinary investments. A serious critique of the ideological workings of disciplinary perspectives, this work at best locates the problematic of marginality within a discursive setting which compels the construction and regulation of a self/other, presence/absence, center/margin opposition.

Yet another, perhaps more serious problem confronts the development of an interdisciplinary, interventionist lesbian and gay studies: that of funding. Currently, funding regulations for graduate students, researchers, professors, and educators alike compel disciplinary investments. Those projects which do not clearly and visibly "belong" to a particular discipline are often left floating somewhere in mid-air. For graduate students in particular, the development of lesbian and gay studies usually occurs simultaneously within the context of established disciplines and paradigms of knowledge. Indeed, how do we go about getting money from funding sources in order to challenge the very root of those structures, the ways in which they organize research, and the means by which they determine how issues are addressed (or not addressed, as the case may be)? Perhaps there is good news in relation to the development of a critical interdisciplinary pedagogy and research: in Canada, for example, the Social Sciences Humanities Research Council has recently responded to this issue by establishing an interdisciplinary committee to evaluate research proposals. In this context, it becomes easier to conceive of the possibility of engaging in interdisciplinary work (and having it recognized as such), as well as developing critical, interventionist perspectives.

Even as we may be situated within the context of a discipline, we need to understand the workings of disciplinary ideology in presenting empirical and theoretical work as "true." As Spivak (1990b) argues,

> It seems to me that there is no such thing as *the* academic, and I think there is a real danger in identifying one's own position with one of these institutional models, and then thinking of *the* academic. But, given that caution, I would say that in one way or another academics are in the business of ideological production; even academics in the pure sciences are involved in that process. The possibility leads to the notion of disciplinary as well as institutional situation, and then to the subtler questions of precise though often much mediated functions within the

institution of a nation state. Thus one cannot canonize one's own discipline and say "I don't have to know, I'm a theoretical physicist," or "I don't have to know I'm a philosopher" etc. Don't canonize the disciplinary divisions of labour. Some of us need to know this. Our institutional responsibility is of course to offer a responsible critique of the structure of production of the knowledge even as we teach it. (p. 103)

As Spivak so rightly points out, we need to critique the structures of the production of knowledge even as we teach those same structures. And as part of this work, we need to remain attentive to the fact that these institutional structures have not only produced knowledge in certain ways, but that they have also constituted us in select (and limited) positions. In this light, it becomes extremely problematic–perhaps even unthinkable–to speak of "lesbians and gay men" in any sort of monolithic fashion. As such, "our" institutional responsibility (as lesbians and gay men) is of course to offer a responsible critique of the structure of production of "us" even as we teach (about) "us."

To deal with questions of "surviving heterosexism in the academy" raises issues and problematics of identity, difference, pedagogy, cultural politics, and self-representation. The strategies for adequately addressing the question, however, suggest that the task at hand is much larger than originally considered. It involves understanding not only how academe marginalizes and constitutes fags and dykes, but how the political, pedagogical, and epistemological assumptions operating within the practice(s) of disciplinary boundaries are themselves exemplary of an epistemic violence which requires that the center be defined in relation to positions of alterity. To strategically employ identity and deconstructionist interventions, and to engage in interdisciplinary work, is to set out to expose–and move beyond–such epistemic violence. In the midst of such work, we can risk asking "What are we in the process of becoming?"

REFERENCES

Escoffier, J. (1990). Inside the ivory closet: The challenges facing lesbian and gay studies. *OUT/LOOK, 3*(2), 40-48.

Hall, S. (1990). The emergence of cultural studies and the crisis of the humanities. *October, 53*, 11-23.

Leitch, V. (1983). *Deconstructive criticism: An advanced introduction.* New York: Columbia University Press.

Spivak, G. (1988). *In other worlds: Essays in cultural politics.* New York: Routledge.

Spivak, G. (1990a). Strategy, identity, writing. In S. Harasym (Ed.), *The post-colonial critic: Interviews, strategies, dialogues* (pp. 35-49). New York: Routledge.

Spivak, G. (1990b). Practical politics of the open end. In S. Harasym (Ed.), *The post-colonial critic: Interviews, strategies, dialogues* (pp. 95-112). New York: Routledge.

Tucker, S. (1990). Gender, fucking, and utopia: An essay in response to John Stoltenberg's *Refusing to Be a Man. Social Text,* No. 27 (Vol. 9, No. 2), pp. 3-34.

The Mark of Sexual Preference in the Interpretation of Texts: Preface to a Homosexual Reading

Arthur Flannigan-Saint-Aubin, PhD

Occidental College

SUMMARY. Since reading is an interaction or confrontation between the reader and the text–an interaction that depends upon the background and perspectives of the reader as well as on the text being read–we can assume that the dynamics of sexuality and sexual object choice will influence how readers ascribe meaning to literary texts. In fact, although other aspects of our identities come into play when we read, sexual identity is unique and central because of the role that it plays in the creation of subjectivity. Specifically, male homosexuality informs and structures the reading of texts. But what does it mean to be a homosexual reader or to effectuate a homosexual reading of a particular text?

That human beings differ, often markedly, from one another in their sexual tastes in a great variety of ways (of which the liking for a sexual partner of a specific gender is only one, and not necessarily the most significant one) is an unexceptional and, indeed, an ancient observation; but it is not immediately evident that differences in sexual preference are by

Arthur Flannigan-Saint-Aubin, formally a research associate at the Los Angeles Psychoanalytic Institute, is Associate Professor of French at Occidental College in Los Angeles. His published work includes books and articles on French and francophone African and Caribbean literatures. He has a particular interest in and teaches a course on the construction and experience of gender.

Correspondence may be addressed to the author at the Department of Romance Languages, Occidental College, Los Angeles, CA 90041-3392.

their very nature more revealing about the temperament of individual beings, more significant determinants of personal identity, than–for example–differences in dietary preference. And yet, it would never occur to us to refer a person's dietary object-choice to some innate, characterological disposition or to see in his strongly expressed and even unvarying preference for the white meat of chicken the symptom of a profound psychophysical orientation, leading us to identify him in contexts quite removed from that of the eating of food . . . (Halperin, 1986, p. 36)

IS IT MERE SEXUAL PREFERENCE?

In critical discourse and in the academy as a whole, the issue of sexual object choice is often considered irrelevant, trivial, or inappropriate. So, most attempts to put homosexuals and lesbians into the curriculum or to put homosexuality into discourse are still problematic, controversial, and dangerous (see Schultz, 1987). In the domain of literary studies and critical theory, this resistance might be attributed partially to the specific (male) heterosexual bias with which the literary canon has been constituted and the bias inherent in the history and psychology that underwrite and subtend critical theory; or this resistance might be attributed to the general, underlying homophobia of the academy as an institution. One must not underestimate the effects of homophobia and heterosexism; but this explanation, at least in terms of literary studies, seems too facile and incomplete; are there no value-free and valid objections to centralizing the issue of sexual object choice?

Indeed the juxtaposition of the two terms in my title, "homosexual" and "reading," in spite of a long tradition of presupposing a relationship between homosexuality and literature and between homosexuality and creativity in general, problematizes both terms and demands clarification and justification. Even if it were immediately obvious that one could "ascribe a person's sexual tastes to some positive, structural, or constitutive feature of his . . . [or her] personality" (Halperin, 1986, p. 36), it is still another matter altogether to assume that the dynamics of sexuality (and sexual object choice) are such that they can be isolated as influencing how readers ascribe meaning to literary texts. There is, however, increasing and convincing evidence that gender does affect the reading and writing of texts. To date there has been considerable research on the issues of gender and writing specificity, for example, as scholars have attempted to identify gender-marked writing. On the question of gender and the interpretation of literature, the evidence presently is still somewhat inconclusive but does strongly suggest that gender also plays a significant role in determining the nature of the interaction between reader and text and thus in determining how readers produce meaning from texts. In both of these areas, studies that have been published so far fail to address fully or sometimes even to acknowledge the complex interrelation between gender and sexuality. Moreover, those studies that do deal specifically with sexuality do so usually in terms of writing specificity. There is an established tradition of examining the works of presumed or avowed homosexual writers, for example, to postulate the existence of a homosexual thematic and/or stylistic. As I shall explain later, although this perspective has definite merit, it might be epistemologically limited and somewhat unpromising critically. The issue of sexuality and the interpretation of texts appears to be especially problematic, and to date it has been a much less explored area–though it might prove in actuality to be critically very promising.

But the question remains: Can and does homosexuality inform and structure language? Is there a homosexual discourse, a homosexual imagination? I propose that there is such an imagination and, furthermore, that it might be more appropriately or more easily located in the reading as opposed to the writing of literary texts. This suggests then that the "sexualization" of reading might constitute an important chapter in the history of literature, sexuality, and subjectivity. This essay begins with the premise that ". . . although we bring to our reading other aspects of our identities, sexual identity is . . . uniquely central" (Kennard, 1986, p. 65). I place the reader, rather than the text/author, at the very center of the critical enterprise; and in so doing, I follow in the tradition of certain feminist critics who place the woman reader at the center of their analyses; and, like them, I too am influenced by reader-response criticism. Like Flynn (1986), I assume that reading is an interaction or confrontation between the reader and an "other," the text–an interaction that depends upon the background and perspectives of the reader as well as on the text. Like Kennard, I shall be asking, though for me it is no longer an implicit question, in what sense is it meaningful to talk about a homosexual reader or a homosexual reading. How in fact might such a reader be defined? Is this category of reader based solely on sexual object choice? How might such a reading process be plotted, explicated? Why does the category, as I am posing it presently, not include women; and does it include all races and classes of men? Is it trans-historical? Can the existence of a homosexual reader or a homosexual reading of a particular text be reconciled with current theories of reading? If not, does it invalidate these theories? What does it mean ultimately to sexualize, as it were, reading–to posit a group of sexualized readers? In other words what authorizes us to postulate and support the idea of a particular group of men reading?

Even if the category itself proves ultimately to be invalid and untenable, it, like that of the lesbian reader according to Kennard, must be posed in the interest of reader-response criticism and gender scholarship in general. This essay can not and does not attempt to resolve or even to articulate fully all these issues; it will attempt to contribute to the discussion by suggesting how and why sexuality (as others have done for gender)–and specifically male homosexuality– informs and structures and perhaps complicates (the writing but especially) the reading of texts. I shall do this by suggesting the role of sexuality in identity formation and in the creation of subjectivity and by indicating how this role differs for men and women. I shall next address more precisely the issue of homosexuality from a psychoanalytic perspective in order to indicate why one can postulate a male homosexual *identity* and why one can situate a homosexual "imagination" in the interpretation of literary texts. Then, I shall turn my attention to the issue of the homosexual reader by proposing a tentative definition, acknowledging explicitly the limitation of such a definition, and by outlining what might constitute two instances of a homosexual reading.

Any attempt to assess the impact of sexuality on reading strategies poses obvious problems because sexuality is fused with and cannot be easily isolated from other aspects of identity such as class or race, for example; any individual homosexual is necessarily a member of a particular social, cultural, or ethnic group. Furthermore, as I attempt to explore the relationship between homosexuality and reading, I realize that the very word "homosexual" comes with a "heavy complement of ideological baggage" that may prove "a significant obstacle to understanding the significance of sexuality" (Halperin, 1986, p. 36) in reading strategies.

The question might be posed: Why isolate homosexuality as a locus of difference? Is it not, after all–as the epigraph to this essay would suggest, merely a matter of sexual preference? Indeed, some theorists conclude that the heterosexual/homosexual distinction is "based not on true difference but on hierarchical oppositions. One term [the heterosexual] . . . posits itself as the primary term and represses the other term [homosexual], replacing it with its mirror opposite, a secondary term derived from itself" (Rabine, 1987, p. 472). Because of this "symbolic law of oppositions," it can be argued that there is no "homosexual" outside of language; he is produced in and through language to constitute the heterosexual's negative. Homosexuality then is a symbolic construction, what Wittig (1983) calls a "branding by the enemy" (see also Rose, 1982); it is a fiction and possesses no meaning when coupled with "reading" or "writing." Quite simply, it could be argued, there is no homosexual imagination, no homosexual reading because there is no homosexual. I concede that the term "homosexual" like "lesbian," is a "volatile, time-bound, *relational* term" (Morris, 1987, p. 473, emphasis added). Therefore, any useful definition, as Morris explains, will necessarily focus not on the individual man but either on the homosexual community that acknowledges his sexuality and therefore that affirms his sense of himself or on the heterosexual community that fears his sexuality and that denies his sense of himself. I propose nevertheless that there exists a homosexual difference and that it is more than mere sexual preference.

Homosexuality, all sexuality, is in fact the merging of the sexual and the nonsexual, and it is this merging that renders it central to identity. Sexuality is a complex of psychic and behavioral phenomena that encompasses (1) *gender identity*, or the consistent experience of oneself as male, female, or ambivalent; (2) *gender behav-*

ior, or the actions that indicate to the self and to others that one is male, female, or ambivalent and, of course, (3) *sexual object choice* that can be designated as homosexual, heterosexual, or bisexual (Baker, 1980, p. 80). Although I do not contend that homosexuality has *de rigueur* a separable, biologic component, I do consider it, as Rabine and others see gender, as "fundamental" and "as grounding the very structures of subjectivity, representation, and language" (Rabine, 1987, p. 472) precisely because sexuality always encompasses more than just sex. Gender differences and differences in sexual object choice–and the two are inextricably linked–may be the "paradigm by which we conceive the particular pattern of difference that shapes our symbolic order" (Rabine, 1987, p. 472). Finally, homosexuality does have a social dimension as well as a symbolic dimension (if not precisely an innate essence) that are coextensive. It is possible to posit the notion of homosexuals as a distinct group without necessarily grounding that difference in nature. One might say that patriarchal culture "produces" the homosexual, that is, it produces positions from which the sexual minority is allowed/forced to speak; it creates or allows for specific modes of homosexuality within its system of social power relations.

But before preceding with a consideration of how homosexuality might inform and structure the reading (or writing) of literature, it must first be established that sexuality does. "For homosexuality presupposes sexuality . . . that is it implies the existence of a separate, sexual domain, distinct from mere carnality, within the larger field of . . . [one's] psychophysical nature–a locus of energies that determine, at least in part, the character and personality of each of us" (Halperin, 1986, p. 36).

SEXUALITY AND IDENTITY

Although homosexuality, sexuality *per se*, is the confluence of biologic, psychic, and social factors, the term commonly refers only to overt sexual behavior and to erotically charged experience. When we think of homosexuals as a separate, distinct group, we usually think in terms of sexual motivation and in terms of the source of sexual desire. Moreover, one can easily overlook the fact that biologic sex (chromosomes, gonads, internal genitalia, external genitalia, hormones, etc.) constitutes but one aspect of sex, which for humans refers also to gender identity and gender role behavior. One can also easily underestimate the fact that sexual behavior, which includes both the choice of object and the nature of activity, can be *fantasied* as well as overt. For if one concentrates on overt sexual behavior, it does appear, in the two paradigms of sexual motivation–the drive or libido theory proposed by Freud (1908) and the appetitional theory as advanced by Hardy (1964), for example–that the question of sexual object is incidental. There is, however, a third paradigm of sexuality, the object relations theory proposed by Ethel Spector Person and others, in which a particular sexual object choice is not incidental and has significant consequences for the very experience of oneself as oneself. In my own thinking and writing on the subject, I have been enormously influenced by Person's (1980) conceptualizations and formulations–many of which are included hereinbelow.

One can adopt a culturalist or a biologic view of sexuality; and if one believes that sexuality is more a cultural than a biologic phenomenon, the argument in support of its importance for identity might seem weakened. Historical or cultural contingency does shape sexuality, but does it account for the central component in the sexual self? The historian might argue against the assumption that sexuality is primordial to identity since "self-identification in the modern sense of a conscious sense of self may not apply to earlier historical epochs at all, let alone self-identification based on sexual practice" (Person, 1980, p. 618). Some psychoanalysts and psychologists also postulate sexuality as just one component–and not necessarily the most central one–in personality development. Freud was the first, however, to theorize and to demonstrate the central role that sexuality plays in mental life. It is an assumption of psychoanalysis that sexuality is inextricably tied to identity and that sexuality has a nature. As Freud explains, it is precisely because sexuality is linked to other motives–it can be used to establish and to bolster self esteem, to relieve anxiety, to consolidate one's sense of oneself–that it constitutes such a force and that it is absolutely central. The psychoanalytic literature confirms further that sexuality structures the way that the external world is experienced and internalized; it calibrates perception and modulates interpersonal relationships; in short, it is deployed in the service of the ego and is crucial in the very creation of subjectivity. Orgasm, sexual gratification, goes beyond pleasure and the reduction of tension. It affirms personal existence, the absolute and "incontrovertible truth" of one's existence; or, as Person (1980, p. 618) indicates, "non-procreative sexuality serves the evolutionary purpose of establishing a 'primary identity.'" And the homosexual is precisely that being who is mired in the myth and the problematic of non-procreative sexuality. Furthermore, in our culture at least, sexuality is the agency for the expression of intimacy, hostility, and, especially for men, it is the agency for the expression of dependency. If one is to argue that homosexuality is crucial to personality and identity or subjectivity and that therein it influences the reading of literary texts, one must proceed a step further to identify more precisely "those mechanisms (in distinction to drive discharge) that account for the central importance of sexuality in psychological life" (Person, 1980, p. 617). One needs to suggest at least how sexuality is mediated through identity and personality and why it has meaning and value for humans in general but specifically for the sexual minority. In this context alone will it be meaningful to talk about a homosexual reader–and specifically about the male homosexual reader–or reading; it is in this context alone that one can understand the implications of cultural proscriptions and prescriptions for the male homosexual.

In the object relations theory of sexuality, as opposed to the libido theory and the appetitional theory, sexual object choice can no longer be considered incidental; it assumes rather an instrumental function in ego formation and personality development. And we may assume that if an individual's sexuality, including sexual object choice, runs counter to the cultural dictates, then it will very likely be constructed and experienced in a way that renders it, as Person and others have suggested, even more determinant of identity. Surely then, the expression of sexuality is even more central for the homosexual in a culture where other anchors of identity–class, profession, region, national origin, etc.–are weak. For any individual, the repression and inhibition of sexuality has consequences for mental health and self-actualization. Does this confirm that homosexuality has an "essence" and that it seeks a particular expression of its "nature"? The familiar nature/nurture debate, is homosexuality innate or learned, cultural or biologic, has no privileged bearing for the present discussion. The clinical evidence confirms that there is a definite *homosexual identity* if not precisely a homosexual nature: For "in some homosexual male patients who enter treatment in order to change their sexual orientation . . . the effective obstacle to change is not the inability to have intercourse with women, nor the preference for sex with men, but the unwillingness to give up a homosexual 'identity'" (Person, 1980, p. 621). Since during the development of the individual, subjectivity and sexuality are merged, they are in effect "nature" to the individual concerned. Surely sexual object choice is not mere sexual object choice; it is not to be underestimated. For even if it is learned, the fact that it can not be readily altered or "un-learned" confirms that the very learning itself must be intimately connected to identity.

Homosexuality and Gender Differences

The homosexual, and specifically the male homosexual, has a particular relation to language, to the self, and to the world that is mediated through sexuality and that is reflected in the very invention of the word "homosexual" and the concept of homosexuality probably at the end of the nineteenth century. My omission of lesbians from the discussion does not suggest that the male homosexual constitutes another kind of norm from which women deviate. But the clinical evidence is very clear, first, that sexuality is linked to gender in males but not necessarily (or at least differently) in females; and, second, that the primacy of sexuality in identity differs for men and for women. In terms of the psychic structures of gender and the structuration of identity, the homosexual man resembles more closely his heterosexual counterpart than he does the homosexual woman: the homosexual male, in spite of his "difference" is still a biological man, and very importantly, he is a socially constructed man, with all that this implies for phallocentrism and patriarchy.

One would indeed expect then that the way that sexuality is integrated into personality and the primacy of sexuality and sexual expression for identity to differ for males and females. In men sexual expression (genitality and orgasm) is developmentally critical to mental health and personality; it is critical to achieving self-worth and autonomy through gender identity. By a certain age, for example, an anorgasmic male invariably shows signs of significant psychopathology. In women no such correlation exists between sexual expression (achievement of orgasm, which is not the same as sensual-erotic stimulation) on the one hand and mental health, personality development, and autonomy on the other: in women gender-identity and self-worth can be achieved in other ways (Person, 1980, p. 619). Sexual expression, again defined as genitality and orgasm, just does not have the same primacy for women. Whereas male sexuality is hypersexuality, characterized by an emphasis on orgasm, on performance and achievement, in women sexuality is hyposexuality, characterized by low drive (low rates of masturbation, the need to link sexuality and intimacy, and the benign results of anorgasmia): "... the female experience of sexuality [appears] ... reactive rather than autonomous" (Person, 1980, pp. 623-4).

Experts continue to debate whether this fundamental difference between the male and female models of sexuality has a biologic or cultural basis. The importance for the present discussion is that the male homosexual emerges with a particular psychosexual and psychosocial profile. Given the meaning, the value, the very centrality of sexuality coupled with the male homosexual's social experience of sexuality as a result of cultural prescriptions and proscriptions, the homosexual difference can no longer be trivialized and reduced to "mere" sexual preference. Although I wish to argue that the nature and modality of homosexual desire, both as a symbolic construction (the homosexual as constituted in and through language) and as a social construction (homosexuality as experienced historically), underwrite and subtend the hypothesis of a homosexual discourse, that is, a particular homosexual relation to language–including what concerns me presently, a homosexual reader or reading–I do not wish either to suggest the *absolute* uniqueness of the male homosexual or to exaggerate the expression of sexuality as the *sine qua non* of his self-actualization and psychic well being.

HOMOSEXUALITY AND LITERATURE

As I have already indicated, there is an established tradition of examining the theme of homosexuality in literature and of examining the works of presumed or avowed homosexual writers in an attempt to identify a homosexual stylistic (see Sedgwick, 1985; Stambolian & Marks, 1979; Woods, 1987). This author/text approach has merit but it is ultimately limited and limiting critically. Sexuality, and specifically homosexuality, is indeed an important locus of difference, but it is a difference more easily discernible, I believe, in the reading and interpretation of texts. There is an inherent danger in identifying the homosexual "text" by looking at the sexuality of the writer and an even greater danger in defining this text by its thematic.

First, identifying the "homosexual writer" is problematic since homosexuality is not genetic or hereditary: a homosexual writer does not necessarily beget a homosexual text. The distinction that Richard Howard (1979) attempts to establish between a "writer who is homosexual" and a "homosexual writer" is interesting but ultimately vacuous. He sees the first as perhaps less worthy of critical attention and he writes that the second is coextensive with his text. Howard does not in fact attempt to establish the components of the homosexual text; but when he writes of the "invisibility of the homosexual writer" whose text can be co-opted by literary conventions, he is suggesting however that the homosexual text is a homologue of the homosexual writer: it parallels, projects, or is in some way mimetic of his psychic or social realities to such an extent that "when the homosexual is no longer the subject of which his book is the predicate" (Howard, 1979, p. 21), then he no longer exists.

Stambolian and Marks (1979), argue, surely inadvertently, against the existence of a homosexual writer or text by affirming that none of the writers examined in their study would likely "accept the label 'homosexual writer' or the category 'homosexual literature'" (Stambolian & Marks, 1979, p. 24). They attest further to the difficulties in postulating the existence of the homosexual text (which they see principally as productions of the homosexual writer) by suggesting that it is possible for the non-homosexual writer to produce a homosexual text by, I would assume, writing "like" a homosexual, just as it is possible for the homosexual writer to create a non-homosexual text: ". . . the works of many writers who never wrote about homosexuality nevertheless contain fantasies, patterns of imagery, or structures of language that some critics have begun tentatively to identify as 'homosexual'" (Stambolian & Marks, 1979, p. 24).

Why then privilege the works of avowed or presumed homosexual writers by looking exclusively or even specifically at how homosexuality may have affected their works and their lives? One rationale for sexualizing, as it were, the issue of writing specificity is the assumption that homosexuals bring to the themes of literature perspectives and values that merit examination. Although it has limitations epistemologically and as a critical perspective, it is useful to undertake a study of the homosexual as writer, a study of the histories, styles, and structures of writing by homosexuals. An explication of the dynamics of homosexual creativity, a history of the individual or collective career, all of this, as Stambolian and Marks (1979, p. 24) and others have suggested, is important to establish a homosexual "typography" that might explain but not be limited to individual texts and individual authors.

It is also important, if limiting, to examine the theme of homosexuality in literature, to examine the inscription of homosexuality in texts in order to deconstruct the political discourse on homosexuality. One question that might be posed: Is there an inscription of homosexuality that is free from the confines of homophobic and heterosexist culture? Historically, the theme has been and still is provocative, "over-determined by psychological and ideological resonances evoked by, but independent of, the text. No doubt there is variation in the intensity and kind of conscious and unconscious charge" (Friedman, 1987, p. 50) that a homosexual "writer" brings to the theme.

Still, the pertinent question remains: If sexuality can inform and structure language, does and how does homosexuality constitute a modality that is independent of theme? Can one expect anything other than a thematic or stylistic from the writer/text-centered approach to criticism? One oversimplifies the issues when one centers

"Gay Literary Studies" on texts produced by homosexuals or in which homosexual experiences are inscribed. The homosexual difference, the homosexual imagination–the "fantasies, patterns of imagery, structures of language" of which Stambolian and Marks write (1979, p. 24)–can also be located in the reader, in the confrontation between reader and text. The homosexual discourse is one that will appear to the imagination in a particular way. It is one that will appear and appeal to a particular imagination. A reader will decode it and connect with it consciously or unconsciously. The distinction between homosexual and non-homosexual discourse, just like the distinction between female and male discourse, "lies not in the [text, language] itself but in the way its final meaning is constituted in the process of reading" (Friedman, 1987, p. 61). In the language of Freud, homosexuality, like all "perversions," is not a problem (neurosis); it is rather the solution to a problem. I contend that one does not necessarily write (problematize) one's homosexuality, but one invariably reads its solutions in and into texts.

What does it mean to be a homosexual reader? Can one learn to be a homosexual reader as some feminists, in Fetterley's (1978) words, have learned to become "resisting" readers? Is this reading too a hermeneutic designed to give meaning and structure to the experiences and perspectives of homosexuals? Does this reading constitute in fact a political stance, an act undertaken to interpret the world and to change "the consciousness of those who read and their relationship to what they read" (Fetterley, 1978, pp. viii-ix)? Finally, is there a distinction to be made between "being" a homosexual reader and effectuating a homosexual *reading* of a particular text. Is this a condition or an activity? Again, I shall not attempt to address all of these issues presently; my subsequent remarks are meant to be preambular; therefore, my paradigms necessarily will be schematic.

The Homosexual Reader/A Homosexual Reading

To displace the focus of the literary analysis away from the text/author *per se* and to refocus it on the reader's interaction with and experience of the text necessitate an entry into the domain of psychology. Reading, as Norman Holland (1975) theorizes it for example, involves both conscious and unconscious processes. On a conscious level, a reader might engage texts for political, social, moral, or other reasons including pure diversion. On an unconscious level, a reader engages texts "for the sake of the pleasure of transforming 'primitive wishes and fears into significance and coherence'" (Miner, 1986, p. 188). On this level, "We can understand the relation between the text and [the reader] . . . through a general psychoanalytic principle. We re-create the text to make it an expression of our *personal style* or *identity*, matching differences and expectations to the text so as to project fantasies into it and transform them and it towards significance" (Holland & Sherman, 1986, p. 231, emphasis added). Of course we bring to the reading process all of the complexities and nuances of our identities, but as the preceding discussion invariably leads us to believe, our sexual identity is unique and central. Moreover, since it can be assumed that homosexuals and heterosexuals, like males and females in a parallel but slightly different perspective, are developmentally different (i.e., they undergo different developmental and relational experiences principally because in our culture individuals are raised by heterosexual parents within a heterosexual model), a theory of reading that denies the possibility or that marginalizes the reality of a homosexual reader or reading can not be considered complete or consistent. For, as I have indicated above, even if we are forced finally to dismiss the category of homosexual reader as invalid or untenable, it must be posed.

Yet some theories that account for the experience of literature in terms of a confrontation between reader and text, a confrontation that depends on the very person of the reader, do seem to assume *a priori* or to conclude prematurely that for the reading process (and for human nature in general) the heterosexual/homosexual distinction, like the female/male distinction, either does not exist or is insignificant. Although some critics, especially certain feminist critics, have "corrected" the male bias of theory by demonstrating that gender constitutes an important locus of difference in the interpretation of texts, they tend to consider gender (as a cultural construction but) without addressing adequately the constituent components of the construction and experience of gender. Heterosexuality is generally considered the universal norm and, as a result, sexuality itself becomes parenthetical to the critiques and sexual object choice becomes muted. It remains to be seen if this heterosexual bias, which mirrors the bias of the psychological and psychoanalytic principles on which the theories are based, invalidates altogether these theories of reading. In other words, what are the implications for reader-response criticism and gender scholarship if there is *and* if there is not a homosexual reader? And finally, can one proceed from a hypothesis of such a reader to the mapping of the actual experience of such a reader?

Some of these questions exceed of course the scope of this essay. Presently, however, I would like to propose a definition, albeit a rather schematic one, of the homosexual reader by suggesting how one might read as a homosexual; I propose, more precisely, to sketch what might be characterized as two instances of a homosexual reading which correspond more or less to the two reasons why readers in general and homosexuals in particular engage texts. The first instance involves a conscious, informed reading, *independent of theme and author*, whose aim is to reread the canon to expose the possible distortions of homophobia and the myths of universal heterosexuality. This instance, a kind of (homo)sexual critique, would not preclude of course an examination of the literary corpus produced by homosexuals and addressed specifically to a homosexual audience. The second instance of homosexual reading is based on the premise that the homosexual reader reads in a way, though not necessarily "determined" by his sexuality, that encompasses his sexuality even if he is unaware of it. This constitutes a kind of non-volitional reading from which one can reconstruct a homosexual textual preference, that fictional space in which the reader can re-live and resolve hitherto unresolved fantasies and fears, free from the punitive and repressive gaze of culture. Finally, inspired by some of the questions implicit in much of feminist criticism, I too shall pose a number of questions that might serve as a point of departure for further exploration.

Towards a Homosexual Critique

In this first instance of reading, the nature of the process depends on how one defines homosexual reader. It assumes that homosexuals are able to be aware of themselves as a group because of certain shared experiences and that one must define the experiences of homosexuals "'not just as a *construct* but [as] something that *constructs*'. . . as an ongoing process by which subjectivity is constructed semiotically and historically" (Fuss, 1989, p. 72). However, and as stated above, whether one views homosexuality itself as innate or learned remains unimportant for a homosexual critique; given the role of sexuality in identity, the causality of homosexuality has no important implications for this instance of homosexual reading. How the reader views his sexuality and if and how it is integrated into his person do, on the contrary, have important implications for this instance of reading. One can of course choose to deny one's homosexuality; and whether this is a social or psychological denial, it has implications for a homosexual critique. A homosexual reader, to borrow Jonathan Culler's (1982) logic, does not necessarily read consciously as a homosexual. Therefore, this instance of reading depends on a positive homosexual identity; and I am assuming that one cannot choose a homosexual identity without being predisposed to homosexuality.

But must the category of homosexual reader then necessarily imply an "erotic" component or can the qualifier "homosexual" be broadened to include an entire continuum of male/male emotional bonds? Although the very word is irrevocably eroticized, I do not wish, on the one hand, to eroticize the category *completely* by limiting it to those men who desire consciously and who actualize genital contact with other men; given the interconnections between gender, sexuality, and identity in males, one would have difficulty in grounding this difference purely in choice of object. On the other hand, I do not wish to minimize or to marginalize sexual object choice and thus all that this entails by broadening the term "homosexual" to encompass any and all men whose primary emotional bonds are to other men (as Kennard [1986] does for the word "lesbian"). *All* men are perhaps potentially homosexual and thus capable of a homosexual reading (or what one might call a "homosexual-affirmative" or "homosocial" reading), but I wish to address presently the instance of the reader who has consciously chosen a homosexual identity with all that this identity implies for social existence.

What follows is not meant to be prescriptive and I do not propose it as a definitive statement on the nature and scope of a homosexual critique. I do wish to suggest that there is a way in which the homosexual reader can reread (and then write about) texts, a way to describe and to inscribe them that does not deny or marginalize his sexuality. This rereading of the canon will make the homosexual reader akin to, yet different from, Fetterley's resisting reader and Kennard's lesbian reader. It will empower the homosexual reader by (re)instating him precisely where literary theory and praxis have denied or effaced his existence. The homosexual reader will refuse to take up the heterosexual readerly positions imposed by the heterosexual text; this rereading of the canon then will render explicit the homophobia and the heterosexist bias in literature and in the discourses on literature–that is, in both the production and consumption of texts. This critical work "can expose the assumptions of universal heterosexuality for what it is, a false assumption" (Kennard, 1986, p. 77). One faces here what Suleiman (1986, p. 142), in a different context, calls a critical timidity: "one does not wish to expose oneself to ridicule or to accusations of belaboring the obvious, tilting at straw men." Yet, the hypothesis of a homosexual reader and reading necessarily modifies our approach to and apprehension of texts sanctioned by the canon and of texts in the periphery of the canon.

This instance of reading, as I have already indicated, is independent of theme. The aim of this reading is not uniquely or even principally to ascertain if the homosexual reader responds in a particular way to homosexuality encoded in texts. This does not deny the validity of studies that seek to explicate how readers decode (or, for that matter, how writers encode) homosexual experiences. But, to paraphrase Kennard (1986, p. 62), if the homosexual reader can appreciate only literature that reflects homosexual experiences, he is likely to be very limited in his reading pleasure and, I would add, in his critical perspective and merit. Any reader can and does enjoy literature that does not reflect his experience, even literature that denies and invalidates that experience (Kolodny, 1980).

This instance of reading then, which would confirm Kennard's theory of lesbian reading, is not postulated on a simple notion of identification. It is not postulated on the reader being able to imag-

ine or read a homosexual subtext in(to) texts when it is absent.
Again, this does not deny that there are necessarily idiosyncratic
readings wherein readers project personal fantasies and images onto
texts. Reading, as the experts inform us, is a complex and dynamic
process that might involve both merging/identification and separa-
tion/ non-identification. The homosexual reader, like the patient in
gestalt therapy and like Kennard's lesbian reader, is a composite of
polarities, of opposites that permit him to be male and female,
homosexual and heterosexual (see Kennard's full account of "polar
reading," 1986, pp. 63-68). During this instance of reading, the
homosexual reader might redefine aspects of himself through
contrast with the opposite aspects in a "fictional other" that he has
temporarily experienced through reading. Polar reading allows the
homosexual reader to enter into any text without losing his identity,
without denying the self. So rather than reject the male heterosexual
text or the female text, the homosexual reader merges with it, finds
something in common with it. This instance of reading, when it is
finally and fully theorized, will clarify the distinction not only between female and male reader but equally between male heterosexual reader and male homosexual reader. This reading will lead
us towards a theory of reading that postulates neither woman nor
homosexual as derivative or marginal. In this instance, the reader,
to repeat, will avoid a normative reading, a kind of heterosexual
impersonation in fact, by refusing to take up the heterosexual readerly positions assumed either by the texts themselves or by extra-
textual commentaries. Again, it is a reading valid for any text, for
any author.

Identifying a Textual Preference

The second instance of a homosexual reading is not entirely
volitional since the homosexual reader, whether or not he denies
psychologically and/or socially his identity–whether chosen or as-
signed–must read in a way, though not necessarily characteristic of
his sexuality, that nevertheless incorporates it even if he is not
conscious of it. For are we not in part at least "subjects constructed
by our experiences and truly carry traces of that experience in our
minds and on our bodies" (Scholes, 1987, p. 218)? And to para-

phrase Scholes, with the best will in the world homosexuals will never be able to read *as* heterosexuals and perhaps not even *like* heterosexuals. The homosexual reader, like every reader, will be drawn unconsciously to particular texts since the ". . . fictional text provides a locus, a space, in which a reader might re-experience and re-work unresolved fantasies and fears that date back to earliest infancy" (Miner, 1986, p. 188). According to Holland, and one finds this idea in Freud's writings, readers exhibit a preference for those texts "that allow the most effective (and, hence, most pleasurable) engagement and transformation of the most primitive aspects of themselves" (Miner, p. 188). Of course, the homosexual reader's preference (like any other reader's preference according to Holland's theory) will not be exclusive; he will be attracted to a wide range of texts, even though certain texts will address more precisely his particular psychic needs and structures.

And once we acknowledge that male homosexuals and male heterosexuals, like males and females, inhabit different psychic spheres that limit and structure imagination, we must expect their language to reflect this to some degree. We must also expect them to manifest different needs, to be programmed for different imaginations, to employ different psychic strategies. Therefore, we must also expect them to prefer and to respond to different texts or to respond to the same texts differently; as there are gender-marked reading preferences, so too there are preferences marked in part at least by sexuality. If one could examine the history of literary consumption, there would be a period (comparable to what Miner shows to be the mid-nineteenth century for women in this country) when homosexuals entered the literary marketplace (as writers but especially) as readers with specific demands and expectations. And, just as there is, as Miner (1986) points out, a "women's story" that appeals more to women than men as demonstrated in the sale of books, there is too a "homosexual story" that repeats itself with some variation and that appeals to homosexual readers. It would be most informative to examine the structure and modalities of this "story" before it adopted an explicitly homosexual thematic in the guise of "gay" literature of the past decades. There are many questions to be addressed: When did this text appear? How does it respond to the psychic needs and structures of the homosexual reader? More precisely, how does the hero and how do the structures of this "story" articulate the concerns, the fears, the fantasies of the homosexual reader?

This is not to suggest that the psychic needs and structures of homosexual readers are unchanging or monolithic or devoid of national, ethnic, racial, or class inflections. To flesh out fully the male heterosexual/male homosexual difference in reading strategies one must deconstruct the homosexual consciousness or imagination in its historical specificity. A comprehensive exploration of the issues raised here will have to address more fully the question of why the homosexual (and why any individual) reads. Finally, to flesh out more fully the male heterosexual/male homosexual difference in reading strategies, one must pursue more thoroughly the differences in developmental and relational experiences of the two, as Chodorow (1978) and others have begun to do for the male/female difference. Since, as Chodorow reports, heterosexual females, because of their own psychic experiences, treat and react to boys and girls differently, they will also, I would add, unconsciously or consciously treat and react to the homosexual and the heterosexual child differently.

What does it mean in fact for desire and for entry into discourse for a homosexual male to be nurtured by a heterosexual female in a heterosexual model? In other words, how does affectional-specific treatment produce affectional-specific personality? How is sexuality a factor in determining how individuals interpret the world, contribute "significance to formal signifiers" (Miner, 1986, p. 189)? To pose what I consider the ultimate question on the relationship between homosexuality and literature, I would paraphrase Stambolian and Marks (1979) by shifting the importance and centrality that they attribute to the writer/text onto the reader and the reading process: In what ways does the reader produce semiotic connections that can be interpreted as homosexual? In what ways does all reading struggle with the polarities of male/female, homosexual/heterosexual? Do all texts invariably impose readerly positions? Is it possible, in other words, that the reading subject constructs the text or does the text always construct the reading subject?

If one is interested in a homosexual relation to language, a homosexual imagination and interpretation, one has much to learn indeed from the work of feminist psychoanalysts and theorists who are addressing these same and related questions. Although we can theorize it, it must be demonstrated conclusively that—as is the case with males and females, and not wholly independent from it—heterosexuals and homosexuals, quite likely treated differently as children, will turn as adult (readers) to different treatments (different stories); it must be demonstrated conclusively that given the same text, homosexuals and heterosexuals "will respond to, cathect with and derive psychic satisfaction from different aspects of the text" (Miner, 1986, p. 189).

* * *

The consistent and persistent tendency to marginalize and trivialize sexual object choice seems endemic and ineradicable. Moreover, any response to this tendency is potentially counterproductive since any response falls into and thus perpetuates the very hierarchy (hetero/homo) and marginalization (of the homo) that it would seek to subvert or to discredit. There exists a danger in adopting any critical stance that attracts attention to a minority voice; such a critique runs the risk of being taken for a manifesto and thus of being disregarded: "It is interesting only to homosexuals" (Wittig, 1983, p. 65). The dominant male, heterosexual ideology would claim that the male homosexual reader, like male homosexual discourse and like the male homosexual himself, is marginal; he is not truly male; he is womanlike; he occupies at best the position of the feminine. The radical feminist and lesbian ideologies, if we render explicit what is implicit in the sociopolitical agenda, would claim that the male homosexual reader, like male homosexual discourse and like the male homosexual himself, is still male and thus phallocentric and mired in the webs of patriarchal culture.

If one insists on a reading marked by homosexuality, one is suggesting in fact that homosexuals are outside of the history of literary consumption and outside of History proper. Thus, my present remarks seem tantamount to affirming that there is only one reading structured or inscribed by sexual preference, homosexual reading, since heterosexual reading is not so structured. My remarks seem to imply that heterosexual reading, on the contrary, constitutes reading in the abstract, the norm, the universal; my remarks seem to imply then that, for the reading process, there is the general and the particular; or, rather, the general and that which is marked by the homosexual (Wittig, 1983). Does homosexual reading constitute the mark of sexual preference in the interpretation of texts? On the contrary, there is no neutral, un-marked reading. Given the nature of sexuality, gender, and identity, this is not the only reader nor the only reading for whom and for which sexual object choice is a factor. All male reading and quite possibly *all* reading bears the mark of sexuality; only one is forced, however, to proclaim itself as being so marked.

POSTSCRIPT

Finally, one might constate that this essay, rather than challenging the heterosexual/homosexual binarism, leaves it ultimately enthroned, thereby reaffirming and perpetuating this essentialist antithesis. Have I not therein fallen for heterosexism's ultimate ruse by acquiescing to an imposed minority status and by relegating the homosexual to the status of "other"? To the extent that my postulation of the homosexual reader reinforces certain traditional notions of the homo/hetero difference, does it not foster another form of heterosexist oppression? Yet to insist, as some post-structuralists might do, that the homosexual is a fiction produced through and in language, is to suggest that the oppression of homosexuals is a non-issue: Since they do not exist, a revindication of their rights merely perpetuates the myth of their existence. One way to think through this problematic–at least provisionally–is, to paraphrase De Lauretis (1989), to conceive the homosexual reader not foremost as possessing a set of objectively identifiable attributes but rather as *positionality*, a position within the academy and within the culture at large. The homosexual reader is a position from which a gay oppositional consciousness and politics can emerge. When reading homosexually, we "take up a position, a point of perspective, from which to interpret or (re)construct values and meanings" (De Lauretis, 1989, p. 11). Even if one rejects the notion of a homosexual identity or imagination that is ahistorical or universal and even if one insists on a homosexual subject as nonessential and formed by historical experience and cultural contingencies, one can still analytically claim sexuality as an important locus of difference by taking sexuality as a position from which to read (and act) politically.

This postscriptive shift from the employment of "homosexual" as an essentialist, psychic, symbolic construct to its employment as a non-essentialist, culturally contingent, political one is not fortuitous. It is my assumption that to read within the Academy—as well as to write and to speak—is already and always to take a political stance; it constitutes a conscious act undertaken to interpret and change the world. Thus a homosexual reading finds its place in a general *gay theory* which includes critical discourses on the institutions and representations of a heterosexist society.

REFERENCES

Baker, S. W. (1980). Biological influences on human sex and gender. *Signs, 6,* 80-96.

Chodorow, N. (1978). *The reproduction of mothering: Psychoanalysis and the sociology of gender.* Berkeley: The University of California Press.

Culler, J. (1982). *On Deconstruction.* Ithaca: Cornell University Press.

De Lauretis, T. (1989). The essence of the triangle or, taking the risk of essentialism seriously: Feminist theory in Italy, the U.S., and Britain. *Differences, 1,* 3-33.

Fetterley, J. (1978). *The resisting reader: A feminist approach to American fiction.* Bloomington: Indiana University Press.

Flynn, E. A. (1986). Gender and reading. In E. A. Flynn & P. P. Schweickart (Eds.), *Gender and reading: Essays on readers, texts and contexts* (pp. 267-288). Baltimore: Johns Hopkins University Press.

Freud, S. (1908). *Three contributions to the theory of sex* (Trans., A. A. Brill) (1962). New York: Dutton.

Friedman, S. S. (1987). Creativity and the childbirth metaphor: Gender differences in literary discourse. *Feminist Studies, 13,* 5-23.

Fuss, D. (1989). Reading like a feminist. *Differences, 1,* 77-92.

Halperin D. M. (1986). One hundred years of homosexuality. *Diacritics, 16,* 34-45.

Hardy, K. R. (1964). An appetitional theory of sexual motivation. *Psychological Review, 71,* 1-18.

Holland, N. N. (1975). *The dynamics of literary response.* New York: Norton.

Holland, N. N., & L. F. Sherman (1986). Gothic Possibilities. In E. A. Flynn &

P. P. Schweickard (Eds.), *Gender and reading* (pp. 215-233). Baltimore: Johns Hopkins University Press.

Howard, R. (1979). Preface: Considerations of a transfuge. In G. Stambolian & E. Marks (Eds.), *Homosexualities and French Literature* (pp. 11-22). Ithaca: Cornell University Press.

Kennard, J. E. (1986). Ourself behind ourself: A theory for lesbian readers. In E. A. Flynn & P. P. Schweickart (Eds.), *Gender and reading: Essays on readers, texts and contexts* (pp. 63-80). Baltimore: Johns Hopkins University Press.

Kolodny, A. (1980). Dancing through the minefield. *Feminist Studies, 6,* 1-25.

Miner, M. M. (1986). Guaranteed to please: Twentieth-Century American women's best sellers. In E. A. Flynn & P. P. Schweickard (Eds.), *Gender and reading* (pp. 187-211). Baltimore: Johns Hopkins University Press.

Morris, A. (1987). Locutions and locations: More feminist theory and practice, 1985. *College English, 49,* 465-475.

Person, E. S. (1980). Sexuality as the mainstay of identity: Psychoanalytic perspectives. *Signs, 5,* 605-630.

Rabine, L. W. (1987). No lost paradise: Social gender and symbolic gender in the writing of Maxine Hong Kingston. *Signs, 12,* 471-492.

Rose, J. (1982). Introduction–II. In J. Mitchell & J. Rose (Eds.), *Feminine sexuality: Jacques Lacan and the école Freudienne* (pp. 1-26). New York: Norton.

Scholes, R. (1987). Reading like a man. In A. Jardine & P. Smith (Eds.), *Men in feminism* (pp. 204-218). New York: Methuen.

Schultz, J. A. (1987). Report of the committee on academic freedon. *MLA Newsletter, 19.2,* 18.

Sedgwick, E. K. (1985). *Between men: English literature and male homosocial desire.* New York: Columbia University Press.

Stambolian, G., & E. Marks (Eds.). (1979). *Homosexualities and French literature: Cultural contexts/critical texts.* Ithaca: Cornell University Press.

Suleiman, S. R. (1986). Malraux's women: A re-vision. In E. A. Flynn and P. P. Schweickart (Eds.), *Gender and reading: Essays on readers, texts and contexts* (pp. 124-146). Baltimore: Johns Hopkins University Press.

Wittig, M. (1983). The point of view: Universal or particular. *Feminist Issues, 3,* 63-67.

Woods, G. (1987). *Articulate flesh: Male homoeroticism and modern poetry.* New Haven: Yale University Press.

Teaching Homosexual Literature as a "Subversive" Act

Joseph Cady, PhD

University of Rochester Medical School

SUMMARY. If taught in a way that exposes students extensively and closely to its texts, homosexual literature can "subvert" the long-standing cultural notion that homosexuality is and should remain "unspeakable" and "untouchable." The author's working methods and materials in his gay and lesbian literature courses at the New School for Social Research, where he has been teaching the subject since 1979, are organized according to those principles. His courses also have a secondary "subversiveness" in the present academic climate, in implicitly dissenting from the dominant "new-inventionist" trend in gay studies now.

Teaching homosexual literature can have a healthy "subversiveness" that is fully compatible with solid pedagogy.[1] If taught in a way that exposes students extensively and closely to its texts, homosexual literature effectively undermines the long-standing cultural notion that homosexuality is and should remain "unspeakable" and "untouchable." I have been teaching homosexual literature at the

Joseph Cady teaches literature and medicine at the University of Rochester Medical School and gay and lesbian literature at the New School for Social Research. His published work includes his own poetry and articles on Whitman as a homosexual poet, on AIDS literature, and on the representation of sexual orientation in Renaissance writing. Correspondence may be addressed to: Division of the Medical Humanities, Box 676, University of Rochester Medical School, Rochester, NY 14642. An earlier version of this article was presented as a paper at the second annual conference of the Lesbian and Gay Studies Center at Yale in October 1988.

New School for Social Research since 1979 and in this essay I want to illustrate these points through a description of my methods and materials in my New School courses.[2] I first taught homosexual literature from 1974 to 1976 in the English Department at Rutgers, as one of several founding members of the Gay Academic Union who were inspired by the existence of the organization to start exploring the subject in the classroom; other members giving similar courses at the time in the New York area were Richard Gustafson at Barnard, Arnie Kantrowitz at CUNY's College of Staten Island (then called Richmond College), and Seymour Kleinberg at Long Island University. I have written elsewhere about my experiences in my first courses at Rutgers.[3] This essay continues my exploration of the subject.

The notion that same-sex sexuality is both morally and literally "unspeakable" is one of the longest-standing stereotypes about the subject. Until very recently, it functioned as a largely successful means of "silencing" homosexuality, especially of stifling any widespread and positive public "speech" about same-sex desire. However, as one of traditional culture's chief strategies of control over homosexuality, this stereotype did, appropriately, permit negative speech about same-sex attraction to occur, i.e., when it allowed any expressiveness about the subject at all. The earliest written statement of this stigma that I know of in the post-classical West is Peter Cantor's denunciation of "intercourse of men with men or women with women" as "ignominious and unspeakable" in his twelfth-century tract, "On Sodomy," in which he defines "sodomy" in only a homosexual sense.[4] And earlier in the modern period this notion's longevity was registered glaringly when Lord Alfred Douglas used its language in his ultimately notorious poem "Two Loves," which first appeared in the Oxford undergraduate literary magazine *The Chameleon* in December 1894 and which designates same-sex love as "the love that dare not speak its name" (in contrast to the other, eminently "speakable," love between "boy and girl").[5] Ironically, Douglas' poem helped crucially to make homosexuality more "speakable" at this time, if still only in a negative light, when Oscar Wilde quoted it in his defense in his first trial for "gross indecency between males" in 1895.

The concept of same-sex sexuality as something "untouchable" has a similarly long and tenacious history and is often expressed through the languages of pollution and disease. For instance, in the mid eleventh century Peter Damian pronounced that homosexuality "surpasses all [other vices] in uncleanness; it pollutes the flesh" (from his *The Book of Gomorrah*, in which he gives "gomorrah" only a homosexual meaning).[6] Similarly, in a set of instructions to the Dominican order a century and a half later, Gregory IX called homosexuals (the context makes clear that this is what he means by "the enemies of nature") "more unclean than animals."[7] The same language continued to serve commentators centuries later. For example, in his unpublished draft essay on "Paederasty" (c. 1785), one of Jeremy Bentham's ways of characterizing his subject is as an "infection."[8] Additionally, in the opening pages of their pioneering *Sexual Inversion* (1897), Havelock Ellis and John Addington Symonds repeat both the stigmas I am discussing here in one remark, suggesting how intertwined they were in the popular mind. Ellis and Symonds stress that just "a few years ago" homosexuality "was a loathsome and nameless vice, only to be touched with a pair of tongs, rapidly and with precautions."[9]

The pressure to keep homosexuality "unspeakable" and "untouchable" persists in our dominant society, though the gay liberation movement has of course brought about many positive changes. To contemporary anti-gay forces, homosexuality remains something that should neither "speak" (i.e., by those that feel it), be "spoken about" (i.e., by sympathetic outsiders), nor "touched" (i.e., encountered and understood). I believe that homosexual literature by definition challenges this tenacious cultural mandate and can provide a profound resistance to it when taught according to principles like those I have followed so far in my New School courses on the subject: I start with the minimum necessary conceptual frameworks and base those only on the students' experience and common sense; I focus only on materials by insiders to the subject; I go as far back in history for our readings as circumstances will allow; I choose relatively limited periods of time and concentrate near microscopically on them; and I ground our discussions in close reading of the text.

Students enrolling in a homosexual literature course will often have little preparation for the experience. Since meager academic attention is usually given to the topic, most will never have been in a gay-identified course before. Furthermore, since traditional culture is so heavily invested in keeping people ignorant about homosexuality, most will have had little experience in being thoughtful about the subject, even if they are gay or lesbian themselves. For these reasons, I usually start my courses by trying to establish two fundamental frameworks. The first is a working definition of "homosexuality." Here I try to keep the discussion concrete and experiential rather than abstract and etiological. For example, instead of beginning with questions like "Is homosexuality transhistorical?" or "Where does homosexuality come from?", I might start by asking "How (i.e., by what factors) would we identify or recognize homosexuality in a person/author/text?" or "If you said someone was 'homosexual' or 'gay,' what would you mean by that?" The definition that typically emerges from this discussion, and that is certainly supported by our subsequent discussions and readings, is homosexuality as the de facto experience of same-sex attraction. Within this broad definition, I then focus on homosexuality as what we would now call an "orientation" (i.e., a profound and lasting attraction) rather than homosexuality as only an occasional feeling, since only a deeply-felt homosexuality is likely to spur a distinct homosexual literature. At the same time, I am careful to acknowledge that in its most universal sense "homosexuality" could refer to either an orientation or an occasional desire.

The definition of homosexuality that I follow in the course thus depends neither on acts nor on self-labelling. In its terms, for example, the category of "a homosexual" could include, among others: a virgin whose erotic fantasies are chiefly or exclusively about his/her own sex; someone who has sex only with the other sex but whose erotic wishes are chiefly or exclusively for his/her own sex; and someone who had sex chiefly or exclusively with his/her own sex but still called him/herself "heterosexual." As mentioned, the validity of this working definition becomes only more obvious as the course proceeds, but one of its immediate and foremost values is in helping to thwart denial. One of the most common defenses of people who do not want to think about homosexuality is, of course, to demand evidence of "facts" or "acts" in discussing the subject. A stock objection of anxious literary critics, for example, is the red-herring assertion that "We can't conclusively say that X was homosexual since we have no hard evidence that he/she ever slept with another man/woman." [10] A definition of homosexuality based on de facto desire alone removes the ground for evasive maneuver at once and also gives students a means of addressing it when they meet it in hostile questioners outside the classroom. During this part of the introduction, I also point out to the class the relative recentness of the actual vocabulary of "homosexuality." Though this information is by now common knowledge to many scholars and activists, a surprising number of otherwise informed and interested people still do not know it, including some students interested enough to enroll in a gay/lesbian literature course. In addition, it is of course crucial to reading earlier homosexual literature accurately–i.e., it alerts students not to expect earlier writers to employ the literal terminology of "homosexuality," but to look instead for the inevitable use of other kinds of language for the subject.

The other general framework that I usually try to establish in starting is a working definition of "homosexual oppression." Here my approach is similarly concrete, asking for ideas from the students' experience or their sense of logic. I would of course underscore any specific mechanisms of oppression that came up in discussion–one could certainly be homosexuality's enforced "unspeakableness," for instance–but I try to arrive at as inclusive a definition as possible here. The one that has seemed to make the most sense so far is the notion of gay oppression as any culturally-imposed inequality between what we would now call "homosexuality" and "heterosexuality." This definition is broad enough to cover an entire range of constraints, from the relatively "benign" (heterosexuals may legally marry, while homosexuals may not), to the more confining (in traditional cultures most heterosexuality may publicly "speak"–e.g., courtship, marriage–while no homosexuality may), to the most grave (in societies where sodomy is a capital crime, all active homosexuals would be liable to execution, since all homosexuality is by definition "sodomy," while only some heterosexuals would be similarly threatened).

My chief reason for also discussing gay oppression in the introduction to my courses is, of course, that homosexual oppression has so clearly been the overarching context of homosexual literature.

Grasping its dynamic from the start, for instance, would help students understand the degree of protective coding that inevitably occurs in earlier homosexual writing. An opening consideration of gay oppression also gives further support to the working definition of "homosexuality" I follow in the course. Understanding the pressure that existed in earlier periods to conceal any detectable homosexual activity and to avoid homosexual self-identification further explains why it is necessary to define homosexuality by the presence of de facto same-sex desire alone–for example, that is often the only kind of trace earlier homosexual writers felt safe enough to leave. In addition, to set the immediate context for our upcoming materials, I sometimes include in this part of the course illustrations of an age's oppression of homosexuality from its dominant writings about the subject. For instance, I started the eighteenth-century course I describe below by distributing to the students Gibbon's diatribe against "the lovers of their own sex" in Book IV of the *Decline and Fall* (1788).

After these opening considerations, which need not take more than an hour or two, I turn immediately to our syllabus of readings. Here I include only authors who we know or can reasonably determine were/are homosexual or bisexual and only writings by such authors that express their homosexual feelings or experiences or that are in some way responses to or reflections of the homosexual situation. That is how I think the category of "homosexual literature" should be defined (e.g., resembling the definitions of other "special" literatures, like black literature and women's literature), and, as is evident, I exclude writings by heterosexuals that contain homosexual characters or situations, as well as writings by homosexual/bisexual authors on clearly unrelated concerns. In choosing specific authors and materials, I have tried to go as far back in the history of homosexual literature as my knowledge and teaching situation will allow. Among my offerings, for example, have been courses on eighteenth- and nineteenth-century homosexual writing, with the 1740s as the earliest point I have reached so far. Writers I have covered in those earlier courses are: Gray, Walpole, William Beckford, Jeremy Bentham, Eleanor Butler and Sarah Ponsonby (the "Ladies of Llangollen"), Byron, Platen, Tennyson, Whitman, Melville, Verlaine, Rimbaud, Hopkins, Christina Rossetti, Margaret Fuller, Dickinson, Sarah Orne Jewett, Wilde, Housman, and James.

These are certainly not the only writers who could be covered in such earlier courses. Were I giving the eighteenth-century one again, for instance, I would want to add some of the period's other lesbian or bisexual female writers whom I learned about later (e.g., Charlotte Charke, Elizabeth Carter, Catherine Talbot, Elizabeth Montagu, Anna Seward, Mary Wollstonecraft), as well as some other pertinent male writers (e.g., Winckelmann's letters and essays, Sade); one could also go back earlier in the period to cover other homosexual/bisexual male authors (e.g., Rochester, Lord Hervey). In new nineteenth-century courses, I would definitely add selections from Ulrichs, John Addington Symonds, and Edward Carpenter, all of whom wrote homosexual liberation essays before the Oscar Wilde trials, and I might also want to include (among others) Hans Christian Andersen, Thomas Lovell Beddoes, Gogol, Thoreau, Edward Fitzgerald, Horatio Alger, Charles Warren Stoddard, William Cory, Newman, Pater, and Katherine Bradley and Edith Cooper, the late-Victorian couple who published poetry together under the pseudonym "Michael Field."

I would also go back before the eighteenth century if I thought the situation would favor it. For example, a Renaissance homosexual literature course could be put together from, at a minimum, work by Michelangelo, Montaigne, Sidney, Marlowe, Shakespeare (e.g., the *Sonnets*), Barnfield, Bacon, James I (his letters), and Katherine Phillips, the most distinguished woman poet at the end of the period. But the New School is an adult-education school whose courses run only if there is a large enough enrollment for them, and my experience so far suggests that a period as seemingly "distant" as the Renaissance might not draw enough of the generalist kind of students the New School usually attracts. All of my New School homosexual literature courses have been sufficiently enrolled, but the earliest one I have given so far, the eighteenth-century course, just got the required number. As a companion tendency to this focus on early materials, I have not given courses exclusively on contemporary gay and lesbian writing; so far my sequential courses have stopped at 1956, with Ginsberg's *Howl* and Baldwin's *Giovanni's Room*. This is not because I think contemporary courses are not worth doing; I once gave a half-semester course comparing early and late twentieth-century homosexual writing, where I used selections from Adrienne Rich, Marilyn Hacker, and David Leavitt as contemporary examples, and a course on gay/lesbian writing about AIDS certainly deserves to be offered. But I have assumed that my students might already be more familiar with contemporary gay/lesbian writing than with any other kind and thus might be more curious about earlier and less well-known materials. So far this assumption has proved correct.

As is evident, I have mostly organized my courses by historical periods. Within that framework, I have avoided broad surveys, choosing instead to focus on comparatively short spans of time, whose homosexual writing I then try to document as fully as possible. Enjoying the curricular freedom of a "non-traditional" institution like the New School, I have typically started my courses at whatever point seemed significant to me and moved as leisurely and as fully as possible until the end of the term, where we stopped with whatever year we happened to have reached by that time. For example, in two sequential one-semester courses we started at 1900 and reached the late 1930s and in so doing got an ample representation of the striking amount of gay/lesbian writing in between: e.g., Gide, Renée Vivien, Stefan George, Thomas Mann, Gertrude Stein, Lytton Strachey, Mikhail Kuzmin, E. M. Forster, Amy Lowell, Charlotte Mew, Willa Cather, Wilfred Owen, D. H. Lawrence, Proust, Ronald Firbank, Fernando Pessoa, Nikolai Klyuev, Sergei Esenin, F. O. Matthiessen and Russell Cheney, Radclyffe Hall, Virginia Woolf, Vita Sackville-West, Cavafy, Colette, and Djuna Barnes. Similarly, in two half-semester courses with the common title of "Gay and Lesbian Writing from World War II to Stonewall" we did not get beyond 1956 (as mentioned above), focusing microscopically instead on work produced between the late 30s and the mid 50s by Jane Bowles, Robert Duncan, Carson McCullers, Mary Renault, Paul Goodman, Gore Vidal, John Horne Burns, Truman Capote, Tennessee Williams, Stephen Spender, Christopher Isherwood, Margaret Anderson, Janet Flanner, Sylvia Townsend Warner, Valentine Ackland, Paul Bowles, James Baldwin, and Allen Ginsberg.

Finally, I base all discussion in close reading of the texts. This does not mean that I exclude more general concerns from class exchanges. To get discussions started after students' preliminary reading of the assignments, I have often asked guiding questions like the following, which usually help to frame and illuminate the materials for the class: what is it in these works that allows us to say that they are "homosexual"? (a way, among other things, of further checking the course's working definition of the term); what do they reflect about the situation of homosexuality in their time?; and what are the defining or characteristic processes in them? The last question can of course be particularly compelling for the class, since it can highlight challenges still faced by contemporary gay people. The answer we have found ourselves returning to so far has been the struggle between a simultaneous "self-protection" and "self-invention": "self-protection" in the obvious sense of the need for some degree of masking in the face of an overwhelming hostile society, and "self-invention" not in the sense of the invention of a status that "was not there" before but of the invention of an appropriate language and form for a pronounced and pre-existing sense of difference.[11]

Similarly, I often place the material in historical perspective or stress its own larger historical patterns. For example, when the information is available, I mention major developments in homosexual history that are integrally connected to our readings. In the "World War II to Stonewall" courses, for instance, I helped explain the period's impressive amount of gay and lesbian literature by pointing out the further consolidation of urban homosexual communities brought about by the war and the several major specific breakthroughs in homosexual "speakableness" and visibility at that time–e.g., the Kinsey Reports on male and female sexuality, the foundings of the Mattachine Society and the Daughters of Bilitis, the awarding of the Nobel Prize to Gide in 1947. Furthermore, when relevant I share with the students the larger shifts within homosexual writing that have become evident to me from the entirety of my courses. One of the most striking, for instance, are the marked "bursts" in the amount of gay male writing produced from about 1800 on, with significant accelerations occurring at about fifty-year intervals at first and then at increasingly smaller periods–e.g., about twice as much gay male writing seems to have been produced between 1850 and 1900 than between 1800 and 1850, and then roughly the same multiple again between 1900 and 1925, and so on. Among other things, this pattern would call for more historical attention to the years around 1800 as pivotal in homosexual history (or at least in gay male history) and would support an accumulative understanding of the entire topic (e.g., as opposed to a "rupture" model of it, in which homosexuality first abruptly "speaks" at one particular historical point). Broader concerns and matters like these are too crucial to ignore, but I am careful to maintain the courses' emphasis on close reading by always illustrating or substantiating these general points with concrete textual evidence.

In the aggregate, then, my homosexual literature courses work to provide both extended and concentrated contact with homosexual expressiveness and in so doing intrinsically "subvert" the long-standing cultural notion that homosexuality is and should remain "unspeakable" and "untouchable." In the first place, homosexual "speech" is the entire focus of each course, in keeping with my definition of homosexual literature. Furthermore, by including examples of significantly earlier homosexual writing, the courses expose students to the long history of that "speech." These earlier materials also incidentally support my working contention about the value of teaching homosexual literature in the first place–i.e., in revealing homosexual/bisexual writers struggling to "speak" about their feelings even during eras that were so officially silent about them, they show that resistance to "unspeakableness" has been a fundamental feature of historical gay experience. Finally, by their detailed focus and foundation in close reading, the courses put students in the closest possible "touch" with that homosexual "speech" and, in Ellis' and Symonds' vivid term, work to block any applying of "tongs" to the subject.

Obviously, I prefer these fundamental ways of teaching homosexual literature, but I do not mean that every particular of my approach should or will remain the same. For example, I have felt uncomfortable recently with the relatively minute focus of my courses. This form was a reaction against my very first New School course, where I tried to give a survey of the entire period from 1850 to the present (it was the late 1970s), going from Tennyson and Whitman to Kate Millett and Andrew Holleran in one semester. I felt frustrated by the simultaneously fractured and sweeping structure of this course, where we jumped among a few representatives of at least six discrete moments in homosexual history and literature (late Romantic, early and late Victorian, early modern, mid-century, and contemporary), and I abandoned it the next year for the more microscopic approach I have followed ever since, which seemed to me better to guarantee the concentrated "touch" with the subject that I wanted my courses to provide. However, it has become obvious lately that this microscopic focus usually excludes one crucial element from the courses—the changes that occur in homosexual writing over time (and, relatedly, the larger historical developments reflected by those changes). As presently constructed, my courses instead tend to present varying individual responses to the same single broad set of historical conditions, and I have had to place the texts in historical perspective by a didactic presentation or by referring to a few well-known earlier or later writers my students may have read (e.g., Whitman, Forster, Woolf, Radclyffe Hall, Gore Vidal).

For the immediate future at least, I would like a course structure that illustrates historical change and still promotes close contact with the material. I have decided to try a kind of compromise form that would cover a broad historical span but in which readings would be organized around a major recurring theme in homosexual experience. The structure would be chronological and thus resemble a survey, but authors would be chosen not simply by their accidental place in a sequence of time but by their value in illustrating shifts or variations in the representation of a concern. Otherwise, I would retain my emphasis on earlier rather than contemporary materials. For example, in 1992 I shall offer a course on "The Literature of Homosexual Relationship, 1780-1930," which would cover both literature documenting actual homosexual relationships and literature illustrating the particular frameworks and modes earlier homosexual/bisexual writers adopted when imagining such relationships. I would start with Eleanor Butler's journal about her life with Sarah Ponsonby and end with the correspondence between F. O. Matthiessen and Russell Cheney and between Vita Sackville-West and Virginia Woolf/Violet Trefusis; in between I might include examples from Byron, Melville, Whitman, Verlaine and Rimbaud, Wilde, Sarah Orne Jewett, Housman, and Kuzmin. A similar course that I would also like to work up would be on "Homosexual Liberation Literature," which would focus on the eighteenth century and the nineteenth century before Wilde and would include both frankly didactic materials (e.g., Bentham, Ulrichs, Symonds, Carpenter) and imaginative writings where resistance and liberation are explicit themes (e.g., Beckford, Whitman, Verlaine and Rimbaud). Another could be on "Homosexual Literature and Secrecy," which would cover homosexual writings never intended to be published in the authors' lifetimes (e.g., James I's letters, Symonds *Memoirs*, Sackville-West's autobiographical fragment), homosexual writings later suppressed or bowdlerized (Shakespeare's *Sonnets*, Michelangelo's poems), and published homosexual writings where secrecy is paradoxically a major theme (Whitman's *Calamus* poems); here I would counterpoint those materials with the approved and invariably hostile dominant culture commentary about the subject. Besides allowing for more evidence of historical change, this different course structure might be a more useful model for teachers in more traditional settings than the New School. Limited perhaps to giving a single annual course on the subject, they might need a more inclusive syllabus.

To some gay and lesbian students and teachers, "subversive" homosexual literature courses like mine might at first seem like nothing but good news—for example, in making a long-standing tradition of homosexual expressiveness available for identification, clarification, and support. But this positive value does not preclude stress and conflict. For instance, anyone teaching such a course lets him/herself in for a formidable amount of original primary-source research, since no inclusive anthologies of any period of homosexual writing yet exist and only lesbian writing has been covered in broad survey studies (nothing resembling a comprehensive history of gay male writing has yet appeared).[12] The extent of archeological work necessary to teach my eighteenth- and nineteenth-century courses is obvious, but a similar effort is needed for my twentieth-century courses as well, for, as indicated, I try to go beyond a canon of well-known writers there to include as many pertinent authors as possible.

In addition, courses formulated like mine can bring students some anxiety and pain. This might be especially true if they are gay or lesbian and just coming out, a period when an intense desire to overthrow the effects of oppression is frequently mixed with a defensive wish not to hear anything more about its challenges. For example, the extended and intimate "touch" with the subject that my courses press on students can obviously force them to confront any lingering homophobia they may have, an uncomfortable assessment that can also be especially embarrassing if they themselves are gay or lesbian. Relatedly, my courses' persistent undoing of homosexuality's traditional "unspeakableness" and "untouchableness" could make students think directly about the special features in homosexuality that drive cultures to silence and distance it in the first place. Ultimately, this process might place students in greater conflict with our inherited "heterosexual model" of experience than they are ready to bear–they would have to envision and accept the different kind of culture that would result if homosexuality were permitted to "speak" as freely as heterosexuality, one, for example, where a conception of "nature" based solely on emotional exchange would be as available as one based on biological procreation and where the symmetry and egalitarianism more usual in same-sex bonds would be as much of a model for passionate love as the complementarity and hierarchicalness typical of male-female relationships. Additionally, courses like mine could carry sobering implications about gay and lesbian students' prospects in the present. For example, the history of protracted restriction and suffering indicated by earlier homosexual literature could suggest that they face a demanding and prolonged struggle for liberation. True, the impressive history of resistance also revealed by that literature–e.g., writers' persisting to "speak" despite continuing strictures against it–could also provide fundamental support in that struggle.

To me, however, these risks are clearly outweighed by the "subversive" value of teaching homosexual literature in the way outlined here. Obviously, I would recommend this model to anyone teaching the subject, as both the most faithful and most enabling way to present it. In addition, I want in closing to encourage the use of homosexual literature as basic material in other courses concerned with homosexuality, such as history, psychology, or sociology courses that involve the subject. The kinds of sources that those disciplines usually rely on to study homosexuality are typically external to the experience itself–e.g., law codes, police records, medical texts, a priori theories–and the most "scientistic" branches of those disciplines might bar literature of any kind as a primary source, deeming it, for example, as "subjective," "individualized," "unrepresentative," or "elitist." However, homosexual literature as I define it provides one perspective on the subject that traditional social-science evidence rarely gives–it inevitably places us within homosexual experience and furthermore shows us not just what homosexual people did but what they felt and saw. This quality would of course hold true even for more recent periods when much other information is available–e.g., statistics, mass-media coverage–but it would be even more crucially important for earlier eras whose official, public cultures were notably silent about same-sex desire. With literature's greater potential to express the forbidden than any kind of dominant-culture testimony can, the homosexual literature of those eras is often the only record we have of what the experience of people attracted to their own sex in those periods was like. The same intimate focus and "touch" that make homosexual literature "subversive" in my courses on the subject would make it a crucial primary source in history and social-science classes.

Finally, let me mention one further dimension of my teaching that readers familiar with current issues in gay studies have surely already sensed. My courses inevitably take on a secondary "subversiveness" as well in the current academic climate, for, in both content and method, they implicitly dissent from the dominant trend in the field now, which I have elsewhere discussed as "new-inventionism" and whose best-known argument is that homosexuality is a late nineteenth-century "invention" (e.g., that homosexuality as an orientation placing persons in a distinct existential situation and a distinct relation to society did not "exist" before that time, either in conception or perhaps actually in fact).[13] Whether or not its advocates intend it, this outlook effectively puts bans of "unspeakableness" and "untouchableness" on homosexuality similar to the ones my courses "subvert," bans it then intrinsically works to uphold. For example, the more traditionally "historical" branch of new-inventionism in effect says that scholars or readers interested in homosexuality need not attend to periods before the 1890s (except, that is, to mine them for evidence of homosexuality's "nonexistence" there).[14] As a result, any distinct homosexuality and homosexuals that may have existed before the late nineteenth century would be rendered as "unspeakable" and "untouchable" as traditional culture would have wanted them to be, for an air of modern "silence" will have been maintained about them and modern readers will have been kept "out of touch" with them.

The branch of new-inventionism influenced by poststructuralist literary "theory" would also leave pre-1890s homosexuality in silence, since it too holds that there is no such subject there to "speak" about.[15] However, it would in addition remove all homosexuality from audiences' everyday, common-sense "touch." "History" new-inventionism would seem at least to grant the existence of a solid modern homosexuality that can be plainly recognized and discussed. But with its implication that homosexuality is an essentially "unreal" experiential category (i.e., not just a modern historical "invention" but a cultural "invention" per se), a view it arrives at by imposing deconstructionist concepts like "indeterminacy" on the subject, "theory" new-inventionism implies that even modern homosexuality cannot "speak," be "spoken about," or "touched" with any agreement or certainty. The only possible approach to the subject, this argument implies, is through poststructuralist "theory," which readers must immerse themselves in first before encountering homosexual writing.[16]

Obviously, my teaching conflicts with new-inventionism in basic ways. In content, my courses include earlier materials that would never be part of a strict new-inventionist curriculum, which presumably would be limited to homosexual writing from the 1890s onward. More fundamentally, those eighteenth- and nineteenth-century texts would implicitly question new-inventionism's prevailing historical argument (or at least would press new-inventionism to be clearer about what it means by that argument), since they show numerous men and women passionately in love with others of their own sex before homosexuality was supposedly "invented." In addition, the insistent homosexual "speech" of all the materials in my courses would make it difficult to maintain, as "theory" new-inventionism does, that homosexuality is a fundamentally "indeterminate" subject.

Methodologically, new-inventionism is deductive, starting from sources outside and presumably "above" homosexuality (e.g., earlier law codes, medical texts, deconstructionist "theory") and working down toward the subject from them. In contrast, my courses obviously work inductively, starting from sources within homosexual experience and always referring any larger points about the subject to them. Additionally, in excluding everything but homosexual writing from the syllabus, I clearly assume that homosexuality does not need poststructuralist "theory" to interpret it but instead can speak for itself and is "knowable" on its own simply through students' own experience, intelligence, and common sense. (Besides including only homosexual writing from the late nineteenth century on, the narrow and unchanging kind of homosexual literature course that would follow from new-inventionism's premises would presumably have a deductive form, devoting perhaps as much time to readings from poststructuralist "theory" as from gay/lesbian writing itself and of course having those readings precede the homosexual materials.)

New-inventionism would also seem to extend a less challenging political and psychological experience to students. For example, its implication that no distinct gay oppression existed before the late nineteenth-century (i.e., since no distinct homosexuality existed before then either) could encourage a degree of complacency in contemporary gay people, leaving them with the feeling that they have a relatively short and shallow history of hostility to undo. Furthermore, the implication of "theory" new-inventionism that homosexuality is an essentially "unreal" experiential category would free audiences from having to exercise any alternative cultural imagination when thinking about the subject–i.e., the entire project of envisioning the different kind of culture that might follow if homosexuality were as free to "speak" as heterosexuality would be moot, since there is nothing distinctly and stably "there" in homosexuality in the first place and thus no basic foundation from which such a culture could arise.

Certainly, it is not the purpose of my courses to dispute or "subvert" new-inventionism. I began teaching homosexual literature before new-inventionism emerged and I would teach my courses in the same way whether or not new-inventionism had ever occurred. Moreover, this is not the place for an extended critique of new-inventionism; I have discussed what I see as some of its major shortcomings elsewhere.[17] But it seemed appropriate to mention this difference here in closing, since it would undoubtedly have been noticed earlier by readers familiar with issues in gay studies. It is of course ironic that a method of teaching homosexual literature which seeks to expose students as extensively and closely as possible to homosexual "speech" would be in a minority in gay studies now and might even be declared "unspeakable" and "untouchable" itself if new-inventionism continues its momentum in the field.

NOTES

1. I discuss my difference from contemporary "literary theory" later, but I want to make clear in starting that by "subversive" in this essay I do not mean that term as it is used in academic poststructuralism; for that reason I put the word in quotation marks here. See David Lehman's *Signs of the Times: Deconstruction and the Fall of Paul de Man* (New York: Poseidon, 1991), especially pp. 70, 74-76, and 84, for a critique of deconstruction's penchant for identifying itself as "subversive," a "subversiveness" that Lehman sees as "risk-free."

2. There is of course a problem about whether to title these courses "homosexual" or "gay/lesbian" literature courses. My solution for now is to use "homosexual" for courses on significantly earlier materials and "gay/lesbian" for more modern courses. Relatedly, in my terminology throughout this essay I use "homosexual" when speaking generically or inclusively and "gay/lesbian" for more contemporary matters. Of course, it can also create problems to use any of these terms in a course title when students might fear having them on their transcripts. It is beyond the scope of this essay to address this complex issue, but, as an example of one possible alternative, let me mention a course I gave at Colorado College several years ago. The course focused primarily on nineteenth-century homosexual literature, but included some heterosexual women's literature as well, and I called it "Different Desires in Nineteenth-Century Literature."

3. See my "Notes on Teaching Masculinity and Homosexuality in Literature," *Radical Teacher*, #24 (Fall 1983), 18-21. Reprinted in *Politics of Education: Essays from Radical Teacher*, ed. Susan Gushee O'Malley, Robert C. Rosen, and Leonard Vogt (Albany: SUNY Press, 1990), pp. 154-62.

4. The exact date of "On Sodomy" is unknown; Cantor died in 1192. "On Sodomy" is translated and reprinted in full by John Boswell in *Christianity, Social Tolerance, and Homosexuality: Gay People in Western Europe from the Beginning of the Christian Era to the Fourteenth Century* (Chicago & London: Univ. of Chicago Press, 1980), pp. 375-78; the quoted phrases appear on pp. 376 and 377.

5. "Two Loves" is reprinted in *The Penguin Book of Homosexual Verse*, ed. Stephen Coote (New York: Penguin, 1983), pp. 262-64.

6. Damian's *The Book of Gomorrah* is thought to have been written around 1051. Quoted in Boswell, p. 211.

7. Quoted in Boswell, p. 294.

8. Bentham, "Offenses Against One's Self: Paederasty. Part I," ed. Louis Crompton, *Journal of Homosexuality*, 3 (1978), 400.

9. Havelock Ellis and John Addington Symonds, *Sexual Inversion* (1897; rpt. New York: Arno Press, 1975), p. 35.

10. See, for example, Millicent Bell, "Notes of a Friend and Brother," rev. of *Henry James: Letters. Volume IV: 1895-1916*, ed. Leon Edel, *New York Review of Books*, 19 July 1984, pp. 39-40.

11. I have discussed this struggle at more length in *"Drum-Taps* and Nineteenth-Century Male Homosexual Literature," in *Walt Whitman: Here and Now*, ed. Joann P. Krieg (Westport, CT: Greenwood Press, 1985), pp. 49-59.

12. *The Penguin Book of Homosexual Verse* approaches the entire period from the ancient world to the present in one moderately-sized volume and can only present a few samples from each author. It also mixes homosexual and non-homosexual writers and lacks any scholarly apparatus, including biographical information about authors; it also, of course, excludes fiction and essays. For a longer critique, see my review in *Gay Studies Newsletter*, XI, 1 (March 1984), 19-23. Both Jeannette Foster's *Sex Variant Women in Literature* (1956; rpt. Baltimore: Diana Press, 1975) and Lillian Faderman's *Surpassing the Love of Men: Romantic Friendship and Love between Women from the Renaissance to the Present* (New York: Morrow, 1981) point to a wealth of lesbian writing that could be used in homosexual literature courses. Here, too, however, scholars still have to hunt down the primary sources on their own to decide which ones to teach.

13. For a fuller discussion of "new-inventionism," including why I prefer the term to the more familiar "social constructionism," see my "'Masculine Love,' Renaissance Writing, and the 'New Invention' of Homosexuality," in *Homosexuality in Renaissance and Enlightenment England: Literary Representations in Historical Context*, ed. Claude J. Summers (New York: Harrington Park Press, 1992), published simultaneously as a special issue of *Journal of Homosexuality* 23 (1/2). As I explain in detail there, some new-inventionists locate "the invention of homosexuality" not in the late nineteenth century, but near the start of the eighteenth. Because of constraints of length, I have had to exclude those commentators from my discussion here. The overwhelming emphasis in new-inventionism remains on the late nineteenth century. See two recent and widely-discussed examples: David F. Greenberg's *The Construction of Homosexuality* (Chicago: Univ. of Chicago Press, 1988), and David M. Halperin's *One Hundred Years of Homosexuality* (New York & London: Routledge, 1990).

14. I put "historical" in quotation marks here because I think it is doubtful how historical this outlook really is. As I explain in "'Masculine Love'," for instance, it is based on a strikingly narrow and inappropriate kind of cultural source.

15. I put "theory" in quotation marks here because I share John M. Ellis' view that literary poststructuralism is not a theory at all, in that it precludes itself

from being analyzed and tested on evidentiary grounds. See his *Against Deconstruction* (Princeton: Princeton Univ. Press, 1989), pp. 153-59.

16. For example, this approach pervades the work of Eve K. Sedgwick, who has become the most publicized spokesperson for gay male literary studies at present. As reported in the November 1989 *Lesbian and Gay Studies Newsletter*, Professor Sedgwick's course at Duke is called "Literature and the Invention of Homosexuality." Furthermore, she begins her current book, *Epistemology of the Closet* (Berkeley: Univ. of California Press, 1990), with a long introductory "theoretical" chapter called "Axiomatic" (it takes up one quarter of the volume) before proceeding to discuss a selection of homosexual/bisexual male writers from the late-nineteenth and early-twentieth centuries, all of whom emerged, as she calls it, "After the Homosexual" (the subtitle of her chapter on Melville's *Billy Budd*).

17. See my "'Masculine Love'," passim.

Matters of Fact:
Establishing a Gay and Lesbian
Studies Department

Jack Collins, PhD

City College of San Francisco

SUMMARY. This article describes the establishment and operation of the first Gay and Lesbian Studies Department in the United States. The evolution of instructional services, administrative and student services, and various aspects of institutionalization are discussed. Short statements by two faculty members of the new Department follow the main article.

In August 1988, the Governing Board of the San Francisco Community College District (SFCCD) budgeted monies for the creation of the first Gay and Lesbian Studies Department in an institution of higher education in the United States. In February 1989, after semester-long deliberations in which I did not participate, I accepted the appointment of chairperson of this new entity. By the Fall Semester of 1990, 14 sections of 11 credit classes were offered under the aegis of the Department, with nearly 400 students enrolled.

The SFCCD, though it is at present being entirely reorganized, has traditionally offered credit and non-credit courses through its City College and its Centers Divisions respectively. The new Department was created within the City College Division. City College

Jack Collins received his doctorate in Comparative Literature from Stanford University in 1976. He chairs the Gay and Lesbian Studies Department at City College of San Francisco.

Correspondence may be addressed to: City College of San Francisco, Box L-169, San Francisco, CA 94112.

109

offers two-year Associate degrees in Arts and Science. It trains students for semi-professional and vocational occupations, prepares students for transfer to the California State University, the University of California, and other public and private institutions in California and nationwide, and provides continuing education for non-matriculated students in its Evening Division. City College enrolled 28,561 students in Fall Semester 1990. The total number of students served by City College and the Centers is more than 60,000, or nearly 9% of the population of San Francisco.

An elected Governing Board of 7 commissioners sets policy for the SFCCD. Governing Board members are elected at large in municipal elections, like the Board of Supervisors that is the legislative branch of city government. In 1980, Dr. Timothy Wolfred, an openly gay man, was first elected to the Governing Board. His presence on the Board since that time and his active efforts to identify and service the educational needs of San Francisco's large gay male and lesbian populations have been the primary factor in the creation not only of the new Department but of numerous other resources as well. For example, in 1982, an off-campus center for evening credit and non-credit classes was established at a public middle school in the heart of the largest lesbian and gay neighborhoods. In Spring Semester 1991, the Castro/Valencia program will offer 30 credit and 13 non-credit classes, both general and gay/lesbian identified. Four identified classes will also be offered at nearby Mission High School, which is becoming the second site of a Castro/Valencia Complex.

The Gay and Lesbian Studies Department exists at City College because the institution is the place where the California postsecondary educational system comes directly into contact with both the political system and with, in the broadest sense, the people. Since lesbians and gay men reside in San Francisco in large numbers, are politically well-organized, and support enthusiastically the concept of an educational program focused on lesbian and gay life experiences and cultures, we have achieved the impossible: an academic department, and one that is financed with public revenues.

THE EVOLUTION OF INSTRUCTIONAL SERVICES

City College first offered Gay Literature in 1972, first as a non-credit course at the then-existing Experimental College, then as a special focus English composition class, and finally as a transferable 3-unit English Department elective. Offering this class emerged from the coming out experience of Dan Allen, an English Department instructor and poet. Don Liles and Pam Jones joined the effort soon thereafter. I came on board in 1980, and Dr. Margaret Cruikshank in 1982. Over the years, this literature course proved both viable and durable. It has been offered every semester since it was established.

When I began teaching it, the original 3-unit elective seemed inadequately structured to accommodate the virtual explosion of material being made visible by scholars and of new lesbian and gay writing. Don Liles and I revamped the original course into a 3-unit survey and a 3-unit special topics course. I had the course title changed to Gay and Lesbian Literature. Over several years, I restructured the special topics course into three 3-unit courses on gay and lesbian fiction (American, International, and Contemporary).

The literature courses functioned as lesbian and gay studies courses for many of their students. In 1988, Daniel Mangin, one of those students, tried out the concept of a film course in one of my literature courses, showing five films. A 3-unit film history elective was approved for Fall Semester 1988; more than a hundred students showed up for the first class. Subsequently, following the literature model, a course on contemporary film was approved. Both courses have proved enormously popular and have gained national recognition.

In 1986, Lindy McKnight developed and taught a Women's Studies course on lesbian issues. This course subsequently became a permanent course in lesbian relationship issues. Since Fall Semester 1987, it has been offered every semester to a steady clientele of between 30 and 50 lesbians each term.

In 1987, Edmund Bedecarrax developed and taught a course on the Biology of AIDS. Anthropologist Dr. Mary Redick became the SFCCD's AIDS Education Instructor and designed and implemented a complex and comprehensive AIDS awareness and education program between 1987 and 1990. In 1988, psychologist Dr. George Shardlow, an openly gay man, received a full-time appointment in Behavioral Sciences.

These teachers of the 1980s have provided the new Department with a core faculty. The courses they created and continue to create are now part of a centralized instructional program. It is noteworthy that the new Department began with a fledgling curriculum based on humanities and human services.

Administrative and Student Services

Following his election to the Governing Board in 1980, Dr. Wolfred offered strong support both to the lesbian and gay student group on the City College campus and to instructional, counseling, classified, and administrative staff throughout the SFCCD. An advisory group called the Gay and Lesbian Educational Services Committee (GLESC) formed. Thanks to the efforts of GLESC members, both as a group and as individuals, the aforementioned Castro/Valencia Center was established. As the new Center quickly established itself and rapidly grew, it became apparent that there was a strong interest among evening students in gay and lesbian instructional and counseling services. While daytime classes are desirable, they have been barely viable. The success of Castro/Valencia indicated to me that the instructional services coordinated and developed by the new Department were best targeted initially at the student population served by the Center. At present, daytime students more strongly support gay and lesbian sensitive student services than instructional services, though, of course, the expansion of daytime classes is an intermediate goal.

Over the past several years, lesbian and gay students have had access to several publicly lesbian and gay counselors. The student club has been large, active, and highly visible over the last several years. I hope that City College will move to create an educational service and information center for lesbian, gay, and bisexual students that will centralize counseling and other student services. Such a center could function as an Office of Gay, Lesbian, and Bisexual Concerns and could focus on the non-instructional needs of sexual minority students, including peer support, academic counseling, and financial aid.

By the mid-1980s, GLESC had created a scholarship to honor outstanding lesbian and gay students of the SFCCD. City College has also benefited from the establishment of both a scholarship and an activities fund with monies from the estate of Dan Allen, who died of AIDS in 1985. Six publicly identified lesbian and gay students have been awarded Dan Allen Memorial scholarships since Spring Semester 1989. The activities account will be implemented in the 1991-92 academic year, with several thousand dollars of accumulated interest income budgeted for speakers, audiovisual and print resources, and emergency financial aid for lesbian and gay students. Fundraising in the private sector may well attract gift and bequest monies to support educational services to lesbian and gay students, thus cushioning the City College effort from the cuts and freezes that bedevil public education in general and the California Community Colleges in particular.

ASPECTS OF INSTITUTIONALIZATION

City College has moved cautiously in creating the Department of Gay and Lesbian Studies. Before establishing the Department, it instituted a new minority studies requirement for all graduating students. To receive the Associate degree, students must complete three units in Ethnic Studies, Women's Studies, and/or Gay and Lesbian Studies. The new requirement prudently addressed the issue of strengthening enrollment in minority studies. However, it does not necessarily affect transfer students, who may or may not elect to petition for an associate degree.

The Gay and Lesbian Studies Department functions both as an administrative and as a coordinating entity. My budget includes release time and a small stipend for serving as chairperson, funds for student workers ($4,000 for the 1990-91 academic year), and a tiny supplies allocation. However, although the program enjoys departmental status, I have had to develop curriculum in association with traditional departments, which co-sponsor gay and lesbian identified courses. In addition, hiring and scheduling must be done in association with ''home'' departments on a goodwill basis. Though the College has established new full-time instructor positions in Afro–American, Latin American, Philippine, and Asian American Studies, as well as in Gay and Lesbian Studies, none of the minority studies programs and departments are autonomous at present.

The ambiguous status of the new Department has dictated the development of gay and lesbian curricula within academic disciplines that have traditionally ignored lesbian and gay experience if not directly oppressed us. Thus far the Department has initiated and had approved gay and lesbian identified courses in Anthropology, History, Labor Studies, Interdepartmental Studies, and Theater Arts. We have adapted pre-existing courses in Psychology, Sociology, and Creative Writing and have listed them as Gay and Lesbian Studies classes in the Time Schedule, though not in the City College Catalog. I have developed a job description for a full-time instructor that focuses on the development of courses in the visual and performing arts. We plan to fill this position, the first such in the nation, in Spring Semester 1991; this Gay and Lesbian Studies instructor will assume his or her duties in Fall Semester 1991. Within several semesters, I hope to have in place lesbian and gay identified courses in the various arts, literature and humanities, social and behavioral sciences, and Interdepartmental and Women's Studies.

In addition to establishing beachheads within traditional academic disciplines, it is also necessary to develop Gay and Lesbian Studies as a discipline or as two disciplines. I will be requesting a Gay and Lesbian Studies rubric under which special topics courses and an independent study mechanism can be categorized. I want courses developed in association with local lesbian and gay institutions such as the Frameline International Lesbian and Gay Film Festival and Theater Rhinoceros. I want courses designed to address issues of lesbian and gay life experience, from coming out to youth issues to mid-life experience to the issues of elders. Ultimately, we are looking at the whole person and at consciousness, not solely at subcategories of knowledge, expression, and behavior. To put it another way, we are not only looking at lesbian and gay experience within the context of American life and culture but also focusing on lesbian and gay life and culture itself. It is not enough to add our voices to the academic discourse about ourselves. We must initiate the discourse, transform its terms and bases, and liberate ourselves from the negative aspects of the categories and definitions which, ironically and paradoxically, brought us into existence in the 19th century as an identifiable class of human beings.

Given the present structure of the Department, it has been necessary to work with what is possible institutionally rather than to
proceed from an articulated philosophy. At City College, we must
satisfy "home" departments and the institution at large that our
program is academically "sound" while at the same time developing a curriculum that appeals to the most diverse student population
in the country if not in the world. I am confident that the Department will achieve greater autonomy in the near future. However, I
doubt that we will comprehend what our accomplishments mean,
and, more importantly, what they imply, for many years to come.
Unlike Rutgers and the University of California at Santa Cruz,
which have undertaken surveys and needs assessments and are now
addressing the development of instructional and student services, we
have moved vigorously to develop services but have not as yet
accomplished more than rudimentary surveys. Recent changes in the
City College application form enable students, for the first time, to
request information about instructional and student services to sexual minority students. We are exploring the possibility of tracking
students who request such information and students who enroll in
identified courses in such a way that confidentiality of student records is not violated. The percentage of lesbian, gay, and bisexual
students at City College may be as high as (or higher than) 20%,
and a large percentage of these students are probably "at risk" with
regard to achieving their academic objectives.

As we move gradually toward a philosophy and an overview, I
expect and hope that instructors and students will bring to the Department multiple and various perspectives toward what Gay and
Lesbian Studies is and are. As aware as I am of the powerful institutional resources now available to us, I am even more impressed
by the opportunity to express, define, and argue ethical, philosophical, and political values in the classroom.

One hopes that the establishment of lesbian and gay courses
within the curricula of traditional departments will affect both discourse within disciplines and discourse within the classroom in
positive and enriching ways. Similarly, the creation of new interdisciplinary courses and of links to "mainstream" and community
cultural institutions should facilitate academic adaptation to current
and future community educational needs. Such courses and links

will also recognize the importance to City College itself of the diverse metropolitan world surrounding it. San Franciscans certainly hold the College in high esteem. The Department intends to demonstrate to the lesbian and gay San Franciscans it serves that City College holds their communities and themselves in high esteem as well.

Besides considering the effects of traditional, interdisciplinary, and interinstitutional courses on the general educational discourses about lesbian and gay life, we need to think about the impacts that could be made by courses specific to the experience of distinct groups within the broadly (and politically) defined classification "gay and lesbian." The Department will continue to develop courses specific to lesbian experience and to gay male experience. Since lesbian experience falls within at least three categories (Lesbian Studies, Gay and Lesbian Studies, and Women's Studies), the resources of all three subject areas should be tapped in the development of new (and new kinds of) lesbian specific courses. Given the maturity of the women's movement and of the lesbian movement, a Lesbian Studies curriculum could develop rapidly.

Serving the needs of bisexual students is certainly an imperative, but in the nearer future it will most likely be accomplished within the context of lesbian and gay identified courses.

Generational issues are becoming more apparent with each passing semester. Most of our students are between the ages of 25 and 44, but we are attracting significant numbers of students both older and younger. I anticipate that special topics Gay and Lesbian Studies courses will help us identify the issues specific to different generations within the lesbian and gay communities and will suggest directions in which we might proceed in creating instructional resources to meet the needs of each age group.

Meeting the needs of lesbians, gay men, and bisexual persons of color will be a complex and delicate task, or rather series of tasks. Quite aside from the problems created by racism and homophobia among homosexuals and heterosexuals alike, the phenomena of homosexuality and bisexuality are described and socialized variously in various cultures. Special topics Gay and Lesbian Studies courses specific to African American, Asian American, and Latin American experience are desirable and possible. Ideally, such cours-

es would be co-sponsored by the various Ethnic Studies departments at City College and by Women's Studies. Such curriculum
development would require community input and support, formal
channels for which are as yet undeveloped, although an informal
network is evolving.

However, at present the Ethnic Studies programs at City College
are as preoccupied with the dynamics of racial oppression as gays
and lesbians are with the dynamics of homophobia and sexism.
Homophobia within communities of color remains as rampant as it
is among whites, while racism among homosexuals remains as
intractable as it is among heterosexuals. Homosexuals and bisexuals
of color face double oppression daily, triple if they are female. We
have a long way to go in identifying and servicing the needs of
these students. Neither the Ethnic Studies programs nor Gay and
Lesbian Studies have as yet effectively addressed those needs.

The relationships between Gay and Lesbian Studies and the
"mainstream" departments have thus far proved productive, indeed
often encouraging and supportive. However, while curriculum development has so far proceeded smoothly, problems are emerging
over hiring staff and scheduling sections of identified courses. Such
problems appear solvable, particularly given the movement of ethnic and sexual minority programs at City College toward autonomy
in hiring and scheduling. A larger difficulty may emerge over time
if "mainstream" departments attempt to develop courses with lesbian and gay content independently of the Gay and Lesbian Studies
Department. Given the unusual popularity of the courses we have
thus far developed, it is possible that competition could develop
over the enrollment of the large numbers of potential new students
among San Francisco's lesbian and gay populations. In addition,
given the essential tension between City's non-traditional studies
programs and the traditional departments whose canons have dis-
torted or ignored the experience, history, and culture of ethnic and
sexual minorities, conflicts over authority and authenticity are more
than possible. At present, such conflicts have remained primarily
individual and verbal, as when, for example, another English instructor asked me when I would return to "real" teaching as opposed to providing "therapy" to lesbian and gay students. While
the new Department has thus far enjoyed the respect of the College-

wide Curriculum Committee, to the point that several of our new courses have received praise as models, it is clear to me that a sizeable minority of instructors does not perceive our program as academically "legitimate." Our current lack of autonomy underscores the institution's ambiguous attitude toward nontraditional studies.

While I am entirely confident that we are witnessing the birth of a new academic discipline and that Gay and Lesbian Studies will prove to be extraordinarily successful, I expect that "mainstream" departments will tend to protect their turf and that they may attempt to invade ours. I have already had to thwart an attempt by a traditional department to offer a gay and lesbian studies course without the consent or approval of the Gay and Lesbian Studies Department.

PERSONAL ASPECTS

I never expected that a Gay and Lesbian Studies Department would be created in my lifetime, let alone that I would be the first chairperson of such an entity. I have undertaken this unprecedented task hopefully and wholeheartedly, but I cannot deny that I often have mixed feelings about the consequences of my appointment.

Much of my unease stems from a distrust of the purposes of the educational system itself, which, during my lifetime, has remained resistant to proactive efforts at social and political change. Born to a large Catholic family that struggled to survive economically, I proceeded through private educational institutions as a scholarship student from high school through graduate school. Although I received a superb education at Columbia, King's College Cambridge, and Stanford, I experienced class prejudice often enough that I never felt at home in the elite institutions I attended. While I have come to see my experience at university as extremely valuable particularly because of awarenesses that developed because of such prejudice, certainly I was never as comfortable socially as I was intellectually during my academic training. The riots at Columbia in 1968 and 1970 alienated me as well, because the university, while championing academic and intellectual values and ideals, did not hesitate to use force to protect its political and economic functions and interests. Once I received my doctorate in 1976, I left university life. The environment was not healthy or comfortable enough for me to remain. My experiences as an economically disadvantaged student and, once I came out, as a gay man, decided my departure from university life, though not from the vibrant intellectual life possible in the San Francisco of the 1970s.

After achieving the doctorate, I worked at a rare bookstore in San Francisco for several years as a cataloguer, researcher, and editor of the firm's publications. I became aware of and began to collect gay and lesbian literature and historical documents. I began to review books for a local gay newspaper and to write fiction at this time. In 1978, while remaining a consultant at the firm, I returned to teaching part-time at a local engineering school and at City College. My primary purpose was to gain the blocks of time necessary for a writing career that a full-time office job could not provide.

I was asked to teach City's Gay Literature course as a sabbatical replacement in 1980. When one of my students was gay bashed on a field trip to see a controversial movie (*Cruising*), I became an activist. City College itself was not a pleasant place for homosexuals at that time. I soon found myself giving awareness and sensitivity training to administration and to student counseling services, and though only part-time, agreed to sponsor the lesbian and gay student group on campus. I became involved in Dr. Wolfred's campaign for a seat on the Governing Board.

Although I had less and less time for my own writing projects, I could not forget the bloodied face of my bashed student any more than I could ignore the desperate needs of the lesbian and gay students I was teaching. Given my literary critical graduate training, the prospect of contributing critically and pedagogically to a brand new academic field deeply appealed to me. So, except for a year off in 1984 to write and to travel, I remained. In 1987, when City College abruptly offered upgrades to 24 English and English as a Second Language part-time instructors (in response to a threatened lawsuit), I reluctantly became full-time, entirely unaware that my new status would result within two years in my current assignment.

MATTERS OF FACT

Writing an essay on the Gay and Lesbian Studies Department allows one to articulate certain tentative and personal perspectives that the day-to-day operation of the Department seldom permits. The week I was appointed in 1989, I had to meet both budget and course catalog deadlines for an entity that had just been invented. If the position has given me access to the policy and decision-making bodies at the College, it has also brought all the paperwork of a municipal educational bureaucracy into my mailbox and across my desk. I have been interviewed an average of once a month by the media, including the Associated Press, California Public Radio, and various big city newspapers, though not as yet by San Francisco's major newspapers. Local independent newspapers and the *Bay Area Reporter* have been generous in their coverage. There has been a flood of correspondence and telephone calls from lesbian and gay educators around the country, all of it encouraging and most of it deeply moving. Such support, together with the enthusiasm and dedication of my colleagues and our students, tempers my exhaustion and keeps me motivated as we continue to make academic and political history with every new course and service we create.

Chances to make a positive difference in students' lives have to be seized by educators who believe that institutions of higher education can achieve the ideals and goals to which the academy is ostensibly dedicated. With the creation of the Gay and Lesbian Studies Department at City College, we can now move concretely to meet the needs of sexual minority students who, by and large, have been most shabbily treated by the educational establishment across the board. The impacts of our program on its students are incalculable, but I am confident that they will be positive and empowering. If we can help revitalize the educational system itself as well, correcting the abuses of the past and creating the instructional services of the future, we will have transformed dreams into matters of fact that our oppressors, having invented us in order to control us, could never have imagined.

AN ADDENDUM

I am delighted to include statements by two of my colleagues, who read my article in draft form. Margaret Cruikshank teaches Gay and Lesbian Literature at City College. She is the author of the forthcoming book *The Gay and Lesbian Movement* (Harper Collins). Lindy McKnight is a licensed psychotherapist in private practice in San Francisco. She teaches part-time at City College in the Gay and Lesbian Studies and Women's Studies Departments.

If anyone had told me in 1974, when I first began to connect my lesbian identity with my study of literature, that in less than twenty years many other academics would be doing the same, I would have been incredulous. I was in the closet then. How could I have guessed that one day the study of openly gay and lesbian writers and the study of homosexual themes in literature would be part of my *paid* work in an English department? I had no idea that the exciting intellectual development of women's studies would later be paralleled by another, gay and lesbian studies.

In 1982, when I first taught gay literature, I thought that the choice to do that burned all my bridges to "regular" English departments. Who would hire a dyke to teach Victorian lit and modern British lit? Ten years later, the situation is somewhat different. A grad student or teacher who works in gay and lesbian studies may also have the opportunity to teach in other disciplines *after* he or she shows a professional interest in gay studies.

I feel lucky that during my academic life I have been a part of two revolutions, women's studies and gay studies. While absorbed in women's studies I had no interest in writing by male authors, but involvement in gay studies opened my eyes to new ways of reading. I love the gay subtext of *A Passage to India,* for example, and the work of Isherwood. As a young English teacher, I thought Whitman a bore. When I read him carefully in 1982, I was amazed to be deeply moved by his poetry. Through gay studies, I have evolved as an English teacher.

When I taught a course called "Gay and Lesbian Themes in Modern British Literature" in 1983, I saw myself as a member of a minority group bringing a special focus to a body of literature. I still have that outlook but I also see that because gay themes are so pervasive in Modern British Lit, my course could also be just another "regular" English course.

Before, I thought lesbians and gay men should know the "gay" side of Modern British; now I think any student who wants to understand that period must delve into gay and lesbian subjects.

In the early 1990s women's studies seems strong where it has autonomy and weak where it is subsumed by other programs or included with an array of interdisciplinary courses. The same will probably be true of gay studies. Autonomy and a sharp focus will help it grow; inclusion under an umbrella may dilute its strength. Core faculty are essential. At present, those of us who teach gay studies are self taught. Like the first women's studies teachers, we are creating the discipline.

Margaret Cruikshank, PhD

Why?

I have just read the inspirational article by Jack Collins on the establishment of the Gay and Lesbian Studies Department at City College of San Francisco (CCSF). I am left with that curious mix of sadness and anger familiar to all of those who dream dreams and have visions different from the dominant culture. Along with our rejoicing in this pioneering departmental victory, we must also raise our voices to shout "WHY?" Why is CCSF the *only* institution of higher learning to have a Gay and Lesbian Studies Department? Why are we forced to defend the "legitimacy" of a program that stimulates minds, challenges narrow thinking, and builds up the self-esteem of students, allowing them to question and search and discover in ways not possible before? Why have non-traditional studies always had to struggle for acceptance, inclusion, and enfranchisement?

The difficulty in establishing gay and lesbian curriculum in the colleges and universities in this country is a microcosm of the society at large. It is no coincidence that San Francisco has gestated the first Gay and Lesbian Studies Department. Gays and lesbians are numerous, economically influential, and politically powerful. Yet even here homophobia thrives behind the liberal mask so often covering academic communities. As in the general society, we must fight the pervasive strategy that attempts to divide and thereby conquer us. Limited budgets and political maneuvers begin to pit Women's Studies against Lesbian Studies against Ethnic Studies. Part-time instructors who have created much of the new curriculum find themselves threatened by full-timers who move in to teach their courses to fulfill their required load. Fighting each other for a small piece of the pie obscures the real issue which has to do with why the piece is so small to begin with.

Ethnic Studies, Gay and Lesbian Studies, and Women's Studies are at the cutting edge of higher education. Not only do they offer academic instruction in a myriad of disciplines, but at the same time they reinforce and educate each minority student as to the intrinsic value of their culture and their being. Do we want to turn out roboticized intellectuals or do we want to train our youth to be inspired, global free-thinkers? Colleges and universities should be scrambling to emulate the model City College of San Francisco is offering. Higher education has always held the hope of mankind, and the future of the world. Its job and mandate is to break through bigotry and fear and challenge students to see and understand the world and themselves both historically and dialectically.

Gay and lesbian students deserve the opportunity to have their culture validated and represented. Heterosexuals deserve the chance to understand and learn about gay culture. Being able to embrace and tolerate difference is a mandatory quality for a peaceful world. Students should not have to travel to San Francisco to have this happen. Educators everywhere must begin to develop gay and lesbian curriculum and press for its inclusion into minority departments. Let us make it our goal that a decade from now every major college and university in North America have an established Gay and Lesbian Studies Department. We must continue to ask "WHY?" continue to persevere, and continue to work together with other minority departments. Most important of all, we must never accept "NO" for an answer.

Lindy McKnight, MA, MFCC

Gay and Lesbian Studies in the Netherlands

Gert Hekma, PhD

University of Amsterdam

Drs. Theo van der Meer

Free University of Amsterdam

SUMMARY. Gay and Lesbian Studies have been rather successful on an institutional level at Dutch universities. The article discusses the social and scholarly backgrounds of this development, the work being done, and the societal reception of gay and lesbian studies. The deployment of gay and lesbian studies was possible thanks to the democratic structure of Dutch universities, and to a general acceptance of the aims of gay and lesbian emancipation in Dutch society. The article delineates also the limitations of the Dutch situation, in terms of the "cordon sanitaire" or minority perspective in

---

Gert Hekma is Assistant Professor for Gay Studies at the University of Amsterdam. He wrote his PhD on the medical creation of the homosexual in 19th-century Netherlands and co-edited several collections of essays on the history and sociology of (homo)sexuality, among them (with K. Gerard) *The Pursuit of Sodomy. Male Homosexuality in Renaissance and Enlightenment Europe* (special issue of the *Journal of Homosexuality*). He is now working on the history of violence and homosexuality.

Theo van der Meer is Assistant Professor at the Law Faculty of the Free University in Amsterdam. He is now finishing his PhD on the persecution and the subcultures of sodomites in 18th-century Amsterdam. Earlier, he published on this topic *De wesentlijke sonde van sodomie en andere vuyligheeden* (1984). He is associate editor of the *Journal of Homosexuality* and published many scholarly and journalistic articles on the history of homosexuality

Correspondence may be addressed to Gert Hekma, Institute of Sociology, Gay Studies, Oude Hoogstraat 24, 1012 CE Amsterdam, The Netherlands.

125

which gays and lesbians seem to become enclosed. Also, the future perspectives of gay and lesbian studies are discussed.

In his article about the challenges facing lesbian & gay studies, Jeffrey Escoffier (1990) depicts a widening gap in the USA between "the field's 'new historicists' and the lesbian and gay communities." Whereas a Stonewall generation of scholars relied on the communities, a new generation of academics, apparently successful in institutionalizing lesbian and gay studies in universities, is attuned to literary and cultural interpretations and textual concerns, using a language that bears no relevance to the gays and lesbians in the street and their political struggles.

Almost since their very beginnings (1978) lesbian and gay studies in The Netherlands faced problems not unlike those Escoffier describes, albeit colored by local peculiarities, political landscapes, and personal animosities. For one thing, the social and political organization of homosexuality in Holland is rather different from its counterpart across the Ocean and a terminology like "gay and lesbian communities" does not relate to the actual circumstances in which gays and lesbians live and love or organize themselves politically and socially in Holland. Despite changes in analysis and policy in the late sixties and early seventies in the national gay and lesbian organization COC (founded in 1946) or the movement at large, which to a certain extent were similar to those that Stonewall brought about in the USA, Stonewall only won some symbolic value in Holland after 1977 when the first gay and lesbian parade was organized here in protest against Anita Bryant there. Consequently, it would not make much sense for The Netherlands to speak of a pre- or a post-Stonewall generation or indeed of a Stonewall generation either in academia or politics. The gap, if one there is, runs right through whatever generation there may be, through gay and lesbian studies itself, through political gay and lesbian organizations.

In this article we want to describe the origins, progress, and perspectives of gay and lesbian studies in The Netherlands, drawing on a "round table" discussion we organized with representatives of different programs and on our own experience.

In 1978 initiatives were taken to found gay and lesbian studies (homostudies) in The Netherlands at the Universities of Amsterdam and Utrecht. Their first aim was to change scholarly attitudes towards homosexuality and homosexuals, and to change the way in which homosexuality was represented in academic curricula. Until then only in seminars on psychiatry and psychology was homosexuality discussed, mostly in terms of disease and abnormality. It definitely was not a topic in social sciences, history, or literature, e.g., in courses on Proust homosexuality was never discussed or even mentioned, notwithstanding its importance in his works and his life. The history or the sociology of sexuality had no place in these curriculae because sexuality in general (not only homosexuality) was considered to be a topic of clinical sciences like psychiatry, biology, and psychology. Sexology was a clinical science, and the relevant (international) journals in the field, *Archives of Sexual Behavior, Journal of Sex Research*, and *Journal of Homosexuality*, were definitely clinical journals, oriented towards medicine, biology, and psychology.

This situation has changed dramatically in the last decade. The clinical perspective on sex has become a target of criticisms and next to it, historical and sociological perspectives on sexuality have been developed and today the research in these fields, especially in history, is booming. The *Journal of Homosexuality* is changing its policies and orients itself now more on history and social sciences; and next to the these journals, new ones have emerged, like the *Journal of the History of Sexuality* and *Paidika, The Journal of Paedophilia*. Their emergence cannot (solely) be attributed to gay and lesbian studies (e.g., *Paidika* was founded outside academia) but was part of this more general development to which they contributed and contribute in no uncertain terms.

In the second half of the seventies the policy of the COC, since 1971 called the Dutch Organization for the Integration of Homosexuality, had come under the attack of radical gay and lesbian groups. They held that its sole political purpose had become the integration of homosexuals in straight society and opposed COC's concept of homosexuality as "just the same." Gay and lesbian radicals, like elsewhere in the Western world, favored separatism and a gay and lesbian culture after a fashion of their own. According to them, integration of homosexuality does not mean anything when the concept of homosexuality itself is not given theoretical and practical contents. Tactics of separatism were of course not fully new but known from the black and in Holland more from the feminist movement. As a result of both the critical attitude towards the policy of the COC and of its failure to establish a foothold in other social and political organizations, gay and lesbian caucuses emerged in many different institutions like political parties, unions of teachers, civil-servants, and nurses, in the army and in the po-lice-force. More recently, gay and lesbian sporting clubs started, and public space in parks and around tearooms for gay cruising was claimed. Besides, categorical provisions especially in regards to health problems, were founded or, like the government funded gay and lesbian mental health organization the Schorerstichting (1967), got a stronger hold to answer the ever more intricate needs of gays and lesbians. "Homostudies" was amongst the first of such sepa-rately organized groups in the Netherlands to serve a specific gay and lesbian audience. The COC, gradually adapting to this newly formed social and political landscape, joined the others in their policy of stressing the specific needs and desires rather than the "sameness" of gays and lesbians.

"Homostudies" in The Netherlands were initiated by gay and lesbian students and lecturers from the universities mentioned be-fore. They demanded opportunities for research and education on homosexuality which was nearly absent in the Universities' curricu-lum. Most of the people involved came from the gay and lesbian movement. The Utrecht-initiative was spearheaded by lecturers who had been active in or were sympathetic to the COC, whereas the Amsterdam homostudies was more of a students' initiative, in which members of the radical gay organizations were involved. Rob Tielman, a former secretary-general of the COC, was pivotal in founding the Utrecht group whereas Mattias Duyves and Gert Hekma, from a radical gay group, and the late American Jim Holmes, a leather poet and translator who already held residence in Amsterdam for decades, were the backbones of the Amsterdam group. Both Tielman and Duyves were sociologists, Hekma was an anthropologist, and Holmes held tenure in the department of com-parative literature at the University of Amsterdam.

Other initiatives followed soon, the two most important being to this day the gay and lesbian archive *Homodok* (the *Documentation Center for Gay and Lesbian Studies*) at the University of Amsterdam, and the journal *Homologie*, a bimonthly, now in its 13th year. In both these projects, students from the social, historical, and literary sciences were involved. Besides, the gay and lesbian studies group in Amsterdam and an ad hoc group at the (Protestant) Free University in that city sponsored two of the major international gay and lesbian studies conferences in the last decade: *Among Men, Among Women* (1983) and *Homosexuality, Which Homosexuality?* (1987).

The strategies both groups deployed were not altogether different from those in the USA (De Cecco in San Francisco, Steakley in Madison), Germany (Lautmann in Bremen and Popp in Siegen), or France (Maffesoli at the Sorbonne), yet they probably were successful at an earlier date. In Utrecht the initiative came from already tenured staff, but whereas it seems that comparative initiatives in the USA and elsewhere at least at first remained limited to isolated figure heads (what Escoffier calls the Stonewall generation), they managed to build something of an institute. Like the students' initiative in Amsterdam the Utrecht group won the support of their university council in which students and junior lecturers have some influence, resulting at both universities in the appointment of lecturers specifically for gay and lesbian studies in the faculties of social sciences in the early eighties.

From the very beginning of "homostudies" in Holland, the relationship between men and women, like elsewhere, has for all obvious reasons been a delicate one. Whereas "homostudies," at first very much a men's resort, focussed on sex research, lesbians, more involved with women's studies, preferred to study women's issues. Notwithstanding this tendency, *Homologie* tried and succeeded also quite well in being a joint venture of gays and lesbians. The gay studies and women's studies programs tried to solve the problem by cooperation. This policy has however never been very successful. A better solution was the creation of specific posts for lesbian studies in gay studies. Gradually tensions gave way (though of course they have not disappeared) when it became obvious that questions about sex and identity are closely related to those about gender.

The political and cultural backgrounds of its members influence both the Utrecht and the Amsterdam programs to this very day. The gay and lesbian studies group at the University of Amsterdam in general focusses on fundamental cultural, historical, and literary research and on theoretical issues. The Utrecht group, on the other hand, specializes in applied research–not least of all in regards to AIDS–with direct relevance for the policy makers of the gay and lesbian movement and the government. No doubt the Utrecht group is the more successful one as far as the allocation of money and staff is concerned. Nowadays, approximately 15 researchers work in Utrecht and five in Amsterdam. Also, other universities such as the Catholic Universities of Nijmegen and Tilburg have started "homostudies"-projects.

The obvious differences between both groups gave rise not only to personal animosities (not least of all over the allocation of limited funds) but also to what already in the early eighties became known as the Amsterdam and the Utrecht schools of gay and lesbian studies. In fact they anticipated the acute conflicts Escoffier describes between scholarly interests and the needs of the gay and lesbian communities (or in Holland rather the gay and lesbian movement).

Despite its obvious successes, "homostudies" remain of marginal interest to universities in Holland, a show-piece of good intentions. They owe their existence to a fashionable interest in gay and lesbian emancipation, which has little to do with the scholarly results of gay and lesbian studies.

It may be of some relevance here to point out that the actual political situation concerning homosexuality in The Netherlands is best characterized by a tabu on anti-homosexuality at an institutional level: both national and local political authorities, the press, and the legal system at the very least pay lip service to their support for gay and lesbian emancipation. The government, provincial and municipal authorities provide subsidies for research to support emancipation policies. Within definite boundaries the press provides a representation of "the" gay and lesbian voice and face, and, never shying away from condemning discrimination wherever it occurs, the gay and lesbian institutions at least provide ideological shelter against too blatant a repression. Yet, there is another side to this coin. The present discourse on homosexuality in Dutch society is mainly framed in terms of discrimination and emancipation. Whatever research is done, it is supposed either to level the first or to further the cause of the second. Consequently, fundamental research is usually to a certain extent held in suspicion for its supposedly hidden political agenda and its uncertain results for emancipation.

Taking a closer look at the media representation of homosexuality or lesbianism, one might draw the conclusion that they have virtually become isolated. Gays and lesbians have become a more or less beloved minority, surrounded by an extremely effective *cordon sanitaire* that prevents homosexuality or whatever its consequences from spilling into the rest of society. This is the "minoritizing" perspective Eve Kosofsky Sedgwick (1990) describes in her *Epistemology of the Closet*. The media are best accessible to those–gay, straight, or in between–that either support or acknowledge the existence of this cordon. Moreover, emancipation policies are usually (re)presented as if they are over and beyond discussion, based on a general consensus in regards to wherever society and its minorities want to go to. As a result those gay and lesbian scholars involved in fundamental research are in their turn suspicious of what their colleagues dealing with applied research are up to, blaming them for not addressing any fundamental question as far as emancipation is concerned.

The results of "homostudies" can be appreciated in several ways. Despite what has been said before they, no doubt, helped to pacify social attitudes towards gays and lesbians. On the one hand, its institutionalization is a social move towards the gay and lesbian movement. On the other hand, gay researchers help to inform the public about homosexuality. A general anticipation exists in Dutch society for the outcome of the research. Not only the gay and scholarly press, but also the general press (dailies, weeklies, radio, television) pays attention to their work, and, moreover, the researchers themselves are contributing articles to the mass-media. Political authorities try to turn the results of applied research into definite policy, e.g., in regards to anti-gay and lesbian violence or AIDS-prevention.

At the same time gay and lesbian studies have brought the discussion to a different level. Thanks to their research, more attention is paid nowadays to the (homo)sexual angle in social and historical sciences. "Homostudies," if only gradually, gets incorporated in general sciences. Its research, though hardly its theoretical issues, is cited elsewhere. For gay and lesbian studies this has brought about other fields of interest and to a certain extent also a change of tone and character of research and education. Because homosexuality is not a marginal aspect of social relations, the results of "homostudies" should neither be considered marginal. When we, e.g., discuss homosociality and masculinity, many important social institutions are involved, from sports to politics (homosociality refers to gender-specific, so male-male and female-female relations without regards for their sexual contents).

Already in the early eighties gay and lesbian studies in Amsterdam tried to extend their field into gender studies, or, more specifically, into homosocial arrangements. It was as much an attempt to escape the intellectual and social cordon surrounding homosexuality in Dutch society, as to provide a more firm base for "homostudies" in academia and to link it up with other interests and specialization. This resulted in a major controversy between the Amsterdam and Utrecht programs, and, if more concealed, between gay and women's studies in Amsterdam. The aim of the Amsterdam group was explicitly to move beyond a discourse of emancipation, drawing on Foucault's thesis on "the making of the modern homosexual." If "the homosexual" was a historical creation, whose emergence was to be situated in the 19th century, then his or her identity might not last forever. To get hold in historical and sociological analysis of this "creation," a broader conceptualization was needed. The concept of "homosocial arrangements" would cover the field of both sexuality and gender.

To a large extent this was a scholarly move rather than sensible political strategy to establish "homostudies," or for that matter, women's studies. Such an endeavour needs scholarly support, which is rarely available, while it passes beyond the fashionable interest in homosexual emancipation of university bureaucracies. Scholarly interests are in general beyond their capacities and imagination. The conflicts between the different gay and lesbian studies programs originated in this problem. Hesitations about the university strate-

gies, and also fear to disappear again in male and straight dominated research and education, impede the development of a broader
field like sex and gender for gay and women's studies. Moreover,
many people criticized the concept of "homosocial arrangement"
as favoring reactionary male-chauvinism among the military, in
economy, politics, or sports. Indeed such chauvinism exists within
such arrangements, yet that does not mean that either the researcher
or his or her research is in its favor.

"Homostudies" in Holland emerged because gays and lesbians,
homosexuality and lesbianism got little if any attention at all. Nowadays it gets limited support and critical acclaim. Changes in societal relations over the last two decades provided gay and lesbian
emancipation with a small foothold in politics and elsewhere and
gave rise to a need for scholarly research on a practical, political,
and theoretical level. "Homostudies" defined a domain for research
and education, yet as in other disciplines there has hardly been any
fundamental discussion for its *raison d'être*. How does its field
relate to social or other sciences which themselves do not have (and
neither are able to develop) definitions or a basis for their domains?
The development of sciences has no strict logic, but depends on
rather accidental interests and breakthroughs. "Homostudies" has
a strong political flavor, yet to a large extent that is true for other
disciplines as well. The difference between academia in general and
such special fields of interest is not in the actual politicization of
the latter but in their explicitness about their political aims.

A strategy to develop "homostudies" has to be effected on this
practical and political level. However, there are two major obstacles
for such a strategy. First, the inflexible and conservative attitude of
the bureaucracies in the universities which blocks renewal of research and education. Second, so far in social and historical sciences little attention is given to topics that might be of relevance for
"homostudies," be it sex and gender or the body. Such themes are
not only of interest for gay and lesbian studies because they could
provide a wider horizon and because of their importance in terms
of explanation or analysis but also to verify whether its insights
have indeed a wider relevance.

In his *OUT/LOOK* article Jeffrey Escoffier maintains that in
order to win funding and support for gay and lesbian studies the

academics involved rather respond to academic and disciplinary standards than to the political and cultural concerns of communities outside the university. He also claims that as an academic discipline it should remain in dialogue with the communities that gave rise to the political and social conditions for its existence. There is of course little new about these tensions. But whereas Escoffier seems to imply that the nature of the dialogue should solely be established by the actual political needs of these communities, the kind of academic research that is carried on and its results may contradict acute or vested political interests. Emancipation may or may not be the aim or the result of gay and lesbian studies, the latter may also alter the course that emancipation takes. New ideas, concepts and analyses of homosexuality and lesbianism, about their history and social meaning, about gender and the body produce different or new political aims, change movements and even communities. Breaking the chains that ghettoize and minoritize homosexuality culturally, socially, and intellectually may be the challenge for gay and lesbian studies in the nineties. Its results might be a surprise to everybody.

ROUND TABLE CONFERENCE ON GAY AND LESBIAN STUDIES

Twice a group involved in gay and lesbian studies met to discuss problems and initiatives pertaining to the field. The group consisted of the following participants:

- Henk van den Boogaard, political sciences, formerly Gay Studies at the Catholic University of Nijmegen, now researcher at the NISSO, the Dutch Institute for Socio-Sexological Research, doing research on queer-bashers by interviewing them;
- Gert Hekma, anthropologist, Gay Studies at the University of Amsterdam, research on medicalization of homosexuality;
- Anja van Kooten-Niekerk, director of the N.V.I.H. COC, the major Dutch gay and lesbian organization, and formerly doing lesbian history research;

- Dorelies Kraakman, historian, Lesbian Studies at the University of Amsterdam, research on definitions of women's sexuality;
- Astrid Mathijsen, Law department and Gay and Lesbian Studies at the State University of Utrecht, research on legal discrimination;
- Theo van der Meer, historian, Gay Studies at the Free University, Amsterdam, associate editor of the *Journal of Homosexuality,* research on the 18th-century subculture of sodomites in Amsterdam;
- Theo Sandfort, psychologist, Gay and Lesbian Studies at the State University of Utrecht, research on AIDS and children's sexuality;
- Riek Stienstra, psychologist, president of the Schorer-Foundation, chairing the meetings.

There have been two meetings, the first on January 25, 1991. The proposed themes for the debate were:

1. The perspectives of gay and lesbian studies with regard to studies of sex and gender, of the body, and of emancipation;
2. Applied versus scholarly research;
3. Education in gay and lesbian studies;
4. Relations between men and women.

On the first meeting we only discussed the first two topics, rather inconclusively. Sandfort and Mathijsen stressed the importance of the perspective of emancipation in research and education, whereas Van der Meer, Kraakman, and Hekma made a choice for a broader perspective, and were very interested in both the themes of sex and gender and the body. Sandfort stated: "The social relevance in terms of emancipation defines gay studies." Van der Meer and Kraakman showed a special interest for a sociology and a history of the body, concluding so from their research on sodomites' desires and definitions of women's lusts. Hekma wished to broaden gay and lesbian studies for strategic and theoretical reasons, because homosexuality is a complex and interconnected theme. According to him, gay studies is marginalized and minoritized, and therefore he is a strong defender of a broader perspective as sex and gender.

Van Kooten-Niekerk stressed the problem of the "cordon sanitaire" as it exists in the Netherlands. The government may subvene some gay and lesbian emancipation work, but it is really a bribe not to bother them, and to stay safely away from the straights in a community of one's own. On the topic of applied or scholarly research (or community versus university interests), everybody believed both should be done in an interrelated way. But there is certainly a problem of the research for which the government is paying. Often scholarly research has no relevance at all for movements or governments, and the reverse is also true.

We decided to continue the round table on March 4, 1991, but then we changed our course and accepted the suggestion to write down first our statements on the present and future of gay and lesbian studies, and then to continue the discussion. But because of many other obligations, most of the participants did not succeed in producing their ideas, so further meetings were canceled, and the round table discussion has to await a better future!

REFERENCES

Escoffier, J. (1990). Inside the ivory closet: The challenges facing lesbian and gay studies. OUT/LOOK, 3 (2), 40-48.

Sedgwick, E.K. (1990). *Epistomology of the Closet*. Berkeley: University of California Press.

Lesbian Studies Emerging in Canada

Carolyn Gammon, Mistress of Arts

Concordia University

SUMMARY. This paper provides an overview of Lesbian Studies in Canada historically and currently. The methodology integrates the factual with personal accounts and perceptions. The first sections touch upon theoretical aspects, including: what is Lesbian Studies, the pros and cons of merging Lesbian and Gay, or Lesbian and Women's Studies, mainstreaming versus creating a separate discipline and the threat of cooptation. A brief historical account traces evidence of Lesbian Studies in antiquity, and in the United States and Europe in recent decades. Reports from various Canadian institutions discuss the extent or lack of Lesbian Studies to date. A section on francophone institutions outlines the grass-roots cultural and political pinnings which are necessary to making Lesbian Studies possible in the academy. The paper then focuses on the Lesbian Studies Coalition of Concordia (Montreal), a student group which has struggled for the first series of Lesbian Studies credit courses in Canada.

Carolyn Gammon is founder and ongoing organizer with the Lesbian Studies Coalition of Concordia in Montreal. She is a writer and activist who works to link the struggle against heterosexism and lesbophobia with combatting racism, anti-Semitism, ablism, classism, ageism and sexism. She is currently challenging Concordia University to grant her a Mistress of Arts for a Creative Writing degree she earned in 1989.

The author would like to thank the following friends and colleagues for their generous help in reading the manuscript as well as research assistance, advice, and support: Line Chamberland, Ellen Jacobs, Roberta Mura, Ina Rimpau, Sharon Dale Stone, Jeri Wine; and all the members of the Lesbian Studies Coalition of Concordia, past and present, whose collective voices are found within.

Correspondence may be addressed to the author at: Lesbian Studies Coalition of Concordia, c/o CUSA, 1455 de Maisonneuve West, Montreal, Quebec, H3G 1M8.

You are attending the graduation ceremony of your daughter, niece, or god-daughter, the year is 2000. The loudspeaker blares out: "Jane Doe, Honours, in Lesbian Studies!" The young student takes the degree in one hand, holds a fist high with the other. She is the first graduate in Lesbian Studies in Canada. The loudspeaker plays a nostalgic eighties tune in her honor: "Rise Up." Lesbians and women in the audience rise up out of their seats, and swinging to the music, accompany the heroine down the aisle. The halls of academe will never be the same . . .

No, you are not dreaming, you are projecting, taking a current academic trend to its logical conclusion. Lesbian Studies, undergraduate, graduate, and doctoral programs are only a matter of time.

Twenty years ago and even today in some institutions, a graduate in Women's Studies was difficult to imagine or even dream of. We now have universities across Canada offering undergraduate and graduate programs in this discipline. For schools which began the process in the early 1970s, it has been a long haul, often taking as long as fifteen years to justify and establish a Women's Studies program in a patriarchal institution. For schools which began the process in the early eighties, it has taken half the time or less. So it will be for Lesbian Studies. The first program may take a decade or longer to establish. With the trail blazed, subsequent programs will flourish.

In 1987, as a graduate student in Creative Writing at Concordia University, Montreal, I had never heard of Lesbian Studies; I had never even conceived of putting the two words together. I was writing poetry from my own lesbian perspective, I was seeking out poets with identifiable lesbian content, researching between the lines for those authors who lived lesbian lives–in short, I was "doing" Lesbian Studies unawares. Four years later, I now know that Lesbian Studies programs already exist in Europe, that Lesbian Studies courses have been offered in the United States since the early 1970s, and in Canada, individual professors have been including lesbian content in curricula and individual students have forged ahead with Lesbian Studies often within hostile disciplines, for years. I have seen the commitment of the Simone de Beauvoir Institute, which houses Concordia University's Women's Studies program, burgeon from offering one half year course in Lesbian

Studies to offering a summer course and ongoing courses in both French and English. In four years I have witnessed Lesbian Studies emerging in Canada.

METHODOLOGY

Looking for lesbians has never been easy; finding us, even more difficult. We have been slandered under such terms as "invert" or "deviant" and more recently obscured behind "women" or even "feminist." Lesbian academics disappear into educational institutions under the titles teacher or professor, lesbian students find their realities unrepresented and their opinions marginalized, Lesbian Studies is subsumed under Women's Studies, Gender Studies, or Homosexual/Gay Studies.

This is a paper which is wary of the institutions responsible for our disappearance even while documenting how they have served, in part, as a culture from which Lesbian Studies can germinate. I write from a student's perspective–that hand which reaches up annoyingly at the back of the class, the voice which says "yes, but . . ." I have not attempted a social science survey of this topic so much as a report from an activist position after four years on the front lines. I have sat through weekly meetings when a student jubilantly declares that she has presented her first essay from a lesbian perspective; and I have read my own lesbian poetry in class, followed the next week by a male co-student bringing in a rape poem to compensate. I have made calls on behalf of the Lesbian Studies Coalition only to hear the secretary cover the telephone receiver as, in the background, the department chair says "Tell her I'm not in." I have had professors come to me and say openly "I want to include a lesbian perspective in my class, do you have resources?" Throughout this time I have carried an invisible tape-recorder and now offer the "transcribed" accounts.

Because, as of yet, there is no nationally coordinated Lesbian Studies organization, it is difficult to know exactly how much Lesbian Studies is taking place without a comprehensive survey. In 1982, on editing *Lesbian Studies*, Margaret Cruikshank acknowledged that "a single book cannot presume to speak for all lesbian researchers'' (p. x). I realized on setting out to write this paper that we are already well advanced past the time when one paper could hope to cover the vast amount of individual and collective work that has already gone into making Lesbian Studies a reality in Canada.

BUT WHAT IS LESBIAN STUDIES?

Comparisons between Women's Studies and Lesbian Studies offer insights into what Lesbian Studies is, and how it will develop. Years ago an ill-informed academic might have asked: "But what *is* Women's Studies, what do you study anyway? Menstruation? Childbirth?" This colleague would now be given an incredulous look and sent to do homework. Similarly, a questionnaire put to students and faculty on the need for Lesbian Studies at the university resulted in the suggestion that we might try the "Health Education department."[1] In 1989, a philosophy professor at Concordia University, suggested we look for lesbian content in his department in "courses in ethics which deal . . . with the moral uprightness or degeneracy of sexual conduct."[2] In a Women's Studies course at Concordia, a professor was asked to read an announcement for a Lesbian Studies Coalition event; before making the announcement she looked up to remark on the poster: "Lesbian Studies? You must mean Sexuality Studies."[3] Clearly there is still some confusion as to what constitutes Lesbian Studies.

A definitive answer would be impossible. Who has ever thought to ask what "Heterosexual Studies" are, and if they did ask, it would turn out that all courses in the humanities, social sciences, fine arts, media studies, urban studies, Women's Studies, etc. have touched upon or focused on some aspect of heterosexual studies. Likewise, Lesbian Studies can be seen as a critical approach to any of these disciplines. Anthropology? The study of matriarchies, of the Amazons, of African women's secret sororities or woman-to-woman marriages (Mays, 1981), Chinese marriage resistance sisterhoods, etc. History? The treatment through time of independent women who did not fit the male criteria for "woman"; the burning of six million witches over centuries; the internment and execution of lesbians in Nazi concentration camps; and the parallel struggle and survival of lesbians during millennia of oppression. Education? How children are taught to assume fixed female/male sex roles and how they are indoctrinated with exclusively heterosexual values and customs. Religious Studies? Comparisons between the survival strategies of religious minorities to those of lesbians; looking anew at separatism as the backbone of community survival; the role of lesbians in the revival of the Goddess. These are a few examples of how Lesbian Studies could be integrated and taught within mainstream disciplines.

Although some mainstream academics may still be scratching their heads as to what would make up the discipline of Lesbian Studies, lesbians and lesbian scholars have been practicing Lesbian Studies for decades, labelled as such or not. Lesbians have been collecting memorabilia from their relationships–letters, photographs, stories of the errant family member, the spinster aunt, passed through generations. Lesbian Archives and lesbian history projects have been active in the United States since the mid 1970s; grassroots lesbian groups have offered discussion series, conferences have been held and specifically lesbian publishing houses have emerged, all with little or no help from academic institutions. Within educational institutions, lesbian academics have been conducting Lesbian Studies subversively, as students and professors. We have been infiltrating a hostile environment, saying the L-word in class, offering students Lesbian Studies essay topics, choosing books for a ''Woman and _____'' course which miraculously turn out to be lesbian-authored. We have directed library budget monies to Lesbian Studies materials, we have encouraged one another to submit articles to mainstream feminist journals or attend conferences so that at least one lesbian perspective will be represented.

It is outside the scope of this article to speak for all the individual pockets of resistance to a heterosexist educational system, but it is these often individual, sometimes closeted, efforts over the past decades which have laid the groundwork for the current trend to institutionalize Lesbian Studies in Canada. Eventually, Lesbian Studies courses will be taught from Black, Jewish, Native, Asian, Latina, and a multitude of perspectives. Analyses of how racism, classism, ageism, or the oppression of disabled people, intersect with those of sexism and heterosexism are being addressed by lesbian scholars and these insights will have an impact on many disciplines.

WHAT ABOUT WOMEN'S STUDIES?

Lesbians and women who were present to see the inception of Women's Studies courses in their universities were undoubtedly excited to think that a female perspective in education, long overdue, was finally being recognized. As year after year of Women's Studies curricula–course titles, book lists, syllabi, teaching perspectives–typically revealed little concern for, or knowledge of a perspective other than that of white, middle-class, heterosexuals, many of the initial enthusiasts had to think again.

A Cross-Canada survey of Women's Studies departments, conducted by the LSCC in November 1987 asked if Women's Studies programs included courses with a lesbian perspective. Of approximately forty institutions polled, nine responded. At that time, York University reported that in one course, the books *The Color Purple* and *Lesbian Triptych* were being used as core texts. The University of Calgary replied that they too had "some" (unspecified) content in one Intro Women's Studies course. The University of Ottawa replied that no courses used any "explicitly" lesbian materials but general feminist theory courses would include a lesbian perspective. Other universities responded negatively. At the time, our Coalition members felt grateful that we had received at least some responses, but as Margaret Cruikshank (1982) wrote in her Introduction to *Lesbian Studies: Present and Future* ". . . we are no longer grateful for tokenism" (p. x). For the most part, Women's Studies programs, like the mainstream feminist movement, have failed to represent lesbians.

A brief "Summary of Conversation" by two lesbian students at Carleton University (Ottawa) in March 1987 outlined the difficulties faced in trying to pursue Lesbian Studies at Carleton.[4] A more comprehensive paper, submitted as an honours thesis by Ellen Faulkner at Queen's University in 1989, showed similar results:

lesbophobia from co-students and professors, difficulty in finding reading material, and nominal mention of lesbian perspectives in class (if at all) in core Women's Studies courses.[5] At Concordia too, Lesbian Studies Coalition members and other students come to the Coalition with horror stories of being told that lesbian viewpoints are "limited," or off topic; professors asked to include lesbian content will provide the class with stereotyped or pathological case studies. One course syllabus was brought to the Coalition's attention where the only mention of lesbianism in the six-page syllabus on "Women and Health" was under "Mental Illness." Lesbian students say that if there is to be any lesbian content at all in most Women's Studies courses, the onus is on themselves to bring it up, and even then, at the risk of being silenced, or being marked down for choosing Lesbian Studies subject matter. The end result is, inevitably, self-censorship.

Almost any lesbian student who has survived or is currently surviving Women's Studies (the above equally applies to other disciplines), will tell the same stories. For lesbian professors the picture is not any brighter; they are discouraged to come out even in Women's Studies departments for fear of not being re-hired or being denied tenure. The system of tenure, which has worked so well at excluding female professors, works tenfold to exclude lesbian professors. Every underground gossip line among academics has a story or two of a female professor being denied tenure track appointments or simply not being re-hired because she was lesbian.

Although there are exceptions to the rule (usually on the part of individual professors), heterosexist Women's Studies programs are not responding fast enough to lesbian scholars' needs. We are offered *a* book on a course outline, or *a* half class during a full year course. We are being offered token representation. For a lesbian in academics who has never put the words "lesbian" and "studies" together, this may seem enough at first. But for those of us who have seen the proliferation of Lesbian Studies in the United States and Europe, who have seen the physical vastness of our herstory at the Lesbian Herstory Archives in New York City, or who simply dream faster than Women's Studies can respond, we are working to develop Lesbian Studies programs to parallel and to complement the already existing Women's Studies programs.

WHAT ABOUT GAY STUDIES?

In Europe, the separation of Lesbian and Gay Studies is not common. The University of Amsterdam funds a *Dokumentatiencentrum Homostudies* (Homosexual Studies Resource Centre), the University of Utrecht has a Homostudies program, there is a Homosexual Studies Centre in Siegen, Germany, the Sorbonne has a *Groupe de recherches et d'études sur l'homosexualité et les homosexualités,* among others. Lesbian, Bisexual, and Gay Studies conferences have been held annually since 1987 in the United States. In Canada, Ryerson Polytechnical Institute (Toronto) has taught Lesbian and Gay Studies together since 1987 and the Toronto Centre for Lesbian and Gay Studies (TCLGS), inaugurated in May 1990, is a further development of this trend.[6]

Lesbian Studies must be promoted wherever it has the chance to align itself. But the problems that exist in aligning with Gay Studies are similar to those already experienced in aligning with Women's Studies, that the "lesbian" of the Lesbian and Gay is co-opted by the more powerful, in this case, male point of view. Most tenured professors are men, therefore, most professors in a position to propose Gay Studies will be men. Gay and lesbian are far from synonymous or even parallel terms (they are often conflated) and likewise, Lesbian Studies and Gay Studies differ vastly in content and analysis; an expert in one field is not likely to be an expert in the other. Although both lesbians and gays have suffered from heterosexism, lesbians face sexual discrimination as females in all the ways women do. It would be naive to think that this power imbalance would not be present when Lesbian and Gay Studies combine disciplines.

Lesbian students are not always happy with combining Lesbian and Gay Studies in the classroom. Lori Newdick, at a York University panel on Lesbian Studies reported on her experiences in a non-credit course at Ryerson Polytechnical Institute (Toronto), entitled "Lesbian and Gay Realities."[7] Although the course was taught by a lesbian and a gay man and equally represented lesbian and gay perspectives, Lori felt that certain inequalities occurred just by placing gay men and lesbians in the classroom together. Most of the gay men in the class had been out a long time and were fairly secure in their gay identities, whereas many of the lesbians were just coming out, were older, or just returning to school. To address this, the class was sometimes split into gender groups which benefitted the lesbians, but the gay men complained!

At the 1990 Lesbian, Bisexual, and Gay Studies conference at Harvard University, Jacquelyn Zita (1990) reported similar discomforts for lesbian students in mixed classrooms, which are not unlike the discomforts female Women's Studies students experience in mixed-gender classes. When asked to split into groups of males and females, one male student wanted to be included as a "girl." At the same conference, Karla Jay (1990) noted that the Modern Languages Association's Lesbian and Gay Caucus only agreed to include the word "lesbian" after years of struggle. (An American trend to rename Lesbian and Gay Studies, "Queer Studies," can be seen as yet another way of rendering lesbians invisible, as "queer" is a term most often applied to gay men.) Jay felt that daycare rights for students, demands for an end to date rape, etc., were more likely to be taken seriously in a Women's Studies department than within Gay Studies. One other presenter, Joanne Glasgow (1990), stated simply: as long as misogyny informs Gay Studies, there can be no question of alliances.[8]

In the Summer of 1989, two tenured gay male professors at Concordia University approached the Lesbian Studies Coalition with two possibilities for a Lesbian/Gay Studies course, either taught together or separately. The debate then ensued within the Coalition whether to jump at the chance of having at least some legitimized lesbian content taught within a Lesbian/Gay course, or to "go it alone" and use the Gay course as leverage to have a course simultaneously taught in Lesbian Studies. We knew that we did not want two male professors, no matter how feminist, teaching the only openly Lesbian Studies content to be taught at Concordia. We also knew that they might get their course and we would not see ours for years. Nevertheless, with the support of the Gay Studies professors, we decided to opt for a separate Lesbian Studies course. In the 1989-90 school year, a 6-credit (full year) course in Gay Studies, film and literature, and a 3-credit course in Lesbian Studies, taught by a part-timer hired from outside Concordia, were offered at Concordia. Despite all efforts at equality, the eventual outcome for the first year of having openly Lesbian and Gay Studies taught at Concordia University displayed some of the inevitable inequalities mentioned previously.[9]

The recent development of a Lesbian and Gay Studies Centre in Toronto (unaffiliated with a university) and the obvious effort by organizers at gender parity, is setting a precedent for a progressive and active site where Lesbian and Gay Studies might pool resources and personnel to develop side by side. "Our goal," states the Centre's objectives, "is to establish a permanent, long-range institution which will secure Lesbian and Gay Studies well into the 21st century."[10] The Centre has set up an endowment fund for awards, conferences, research grants, etc. They publish a newsletter, and have conducted a panel series: "Into the Nineties, Lesbian and Gay Studies in Canada." Jeri Wine, an out lesbian and tenured professor at the Ontario Institute for Studies in Education spoke at the first panel sponsored by the Centre. She said: "I am moved by the desire of Gay Studies academics to work with lesbians . . . lesbians have not had that kind of clear invitation from feminists" (Wine, 1990, p. 12).

WHAT ABOUT MAINSTREAMING?

When Women's Studies first came into being, similar debates took place as to how best to get the discipline off its feet. Should individual Women's Studies courses be offered in applicable disciplines (e.g., Women in Literature, Women in History, etc.) and thereby integrate women's perspectives into the mainstream curriculum? Or should Women's Studies programs and departments strike out, independent of other disciplines, to develop a strong academic base but risk being rejected or ignored by already existing faculties? Or maybe, Women's Studies should try a combination of both . . .

I will not repeat or even try to summarize the vast body of literature debating the pros and cons of mainstreaming Women's Studies into applicable disciplines (see Anderson, 1987, Bowles & Klein, 1983). The debate is still hot and undecided with each side now having working examples to compare–York University being a university which originally offered Women's Studies through a double majors program, and Concordia University which offers a diploma and an undergraduate degree in Women's Studies. The same arguments could be used for and against mainstreaming Lesbian Studies.

From working with the Lesbian Studies Coalition of Concordia for the past four years, my opinion is that separate Lesbian Studies programs, especially where Women's Studies programs already exist, may be the path of least resistance. The Coalition's work in trying to have obvious disciplines such as English or Sociology offer a course in Lesbian Studies have met with dead-ends, even when supplying the departments with course syllabi and the C.V.'s of qualified professors willing to teach! Almost all departments are headed by men, each of whom needs to be convinced that Lesbian Studies is legitimate and necessary. "The Curriculum," no matter how male biased, is said to be sacred; therefore, anything "extra" would require hiring a part-time faculty member (as most departments lack competent instructors to teach Lesbian Studies) and there is no budget for that. Despite these setbacks, the Coalition's original and ongoing mandate is both the integration of Lesbian Studies into existing applicable disciplines *and* the establishment of autonomous Lesbian Studies programs to the Ph.D. level.

As with Women's Studies, when we struggle for the latter option, we inevitably have thrown at us the accusation that we are "isolating" ourselves. Yet, separatist strategies have been recognized as effective and legitimate in nurturing and building cultural identity among Natives, Blacks, and Jews, to name a few (not to mention among white males!). Separate Lesbian Studies programs would provide the intellectual space and intensity for advancing the discipline. Mainstreaming, on the other hand, would provide all students with the right to be educated from a Lesbian Studies perspective as one of many perspectives.

LESBIAN STUDIES HERSTORICALLY

Lesbian Studies have been conducted for millennia the world over. Certainly the literary and philosophical exchanges among

Sappho and her pupils did not spring out of a void, nor end abruptly when she died. Convents and other such female-run societies undoubtedly kept traditions and records of the lives of independent lesbians and women. Chinese marriage resistance sisterhoods kept "Good Books" to pass on the tradition of marriage resistance and the female warrior (Raymond, 1986). Native cultures pass down oral traditions through the generations which tell the world from a female-centered perspective (Allen, 1981). A lesbian separatist tract was written in Germany in the late 1800s (Gronewold, 1990) and lesbian journals flourished in pre-World War I Germany. In short, Lesbian Studies have always been with us.

In recent decades, lesbian scholars have begun to compile this evidence. Susan Cavin (1985), in an anthropological survey, notes sixty-four societies world-wide, from 450 BCE to present, where lesbianism is reported. She finds lesbianism among hunting and gathering societies, in pre-class and pre-industrial societies, literally occurring across all human settlement patterns. Woman-marriage as a social institution has been well documented, one of the best known being among the Dahomey in Africa, but also among Native American peoples such as the Mojave, Navajo, and Inuit (Niethammer, 1977). Another comprehensive account of lesbian presence through the ages and cultures is Judy Grahn's (1984) *Another Mother Tongue* which combines poetry, legend, autobiography, and etymology to document lesbian and gay cultural histories.

Adrienne Rich (1980) investigates lesbian presence in terms of the corresponding patriarchal forces used to repress it: "[Such] a pervasive cluster of forces, ranging from physical brutality to control of consciousness, . . . suggests that an enormous potential counterforce is having to be restrained" (p. 12). One has to wonder if the recent advances in Lesbian Studies will likewise be crushed, dispersed, or hidden, so that lesbians in the future will be as ignorant of their foresisters' struggle as I was only four years ago.

Classes in Homophile Studies were held as early as 1956 in the United States.[11] "Homostudies" are offered at the University of Utrecht in the Netherlands and the program has such support that in 1987, Queen Beatrix named a German scholar to a tenured position in Lesbian Studies (*Hag Rag*, 9987). While we wait for Queen Elizabeth to likewise bestow a tenured professorship in Lesbian

Studies in Canada, we realize that we must work at the grassroots level to achieve what has been a given in parts of Europe and the United States for decades.

The ground-breaking book *Lesbian Studies: Present and Future* (Cruikshank, 1982) documents the personal and political struggles of many of the first brave academics to declare themselves lesbian and claim the right to Lesbian Studies in the academy. In 1982, in Canada, *Fireweed A Feminist Quarterly* (Toronto) brought out a major collection of lesbian work: art, politics, fiction, and poetry (and dyke bar postcard collectables!) under the title of "Lesbiantics." With some articles in French, in translation from French, and in English, by contributors from Vancouver, Toronto, and Montreal, this was the first Canadian anthology to pull together lesbian thoughts and perspectives. A similarly courageous collection was released by *Resources for Feminist Research.* "The Lesbian Issue" (1983) includes articles in French and (mostly) English on Lesbians and Teaching, Lesbian Culture, Personal Politics, Lesbian Theory, book reviews, and resources.

Parallels between Lesbian Studies developments in the United States and Canada are striking. In 1977, the first Lesbian Caucus of the National Women's Studies Association met in the United States. A decade later, the first Lesbian Caucus of the Canadian Women's Studies Association (CWSA) met in Canada. In 1972, at the State University of New York at Buffalo, a Women's Studies course was taught entitled: "Lesbianism."[12] In 1990, the first ever Lesbian Studies course for credit in Canada, with "Lesbian" appearing in the title of the course, was offered at Concordia University, Montreal.[13]

In the United States, courses have been offered such as "The Lesbian in Literature" (Queen's College, CUNY, 1975), "Lesbian Culture" (University of Wisconsin, 1980), or "Heterosexism and the Oppression of Women" (University of New Mexico, 1981). Some of these original Lesbian Studies courses display the pitfalls which plagued the first few years of Women's Studies–syllabi with material drawn from primarily white, Eurocentric, middle (or upper) class perspectives. Others are remarkable in that, despite limited or hidden resources, they included from the outset an analysis by class, race, age, ability/disability, etc. Bibliographies often show a cross-genre selection of sources: readings from small, now defunct, pre-Stonewall lesbian magazines, poetry, interviews, diaries, and fiction. Because no Lesbian Studies texts existed *per se* before 1982, reading lists were often (and are still) more eclectic and comprehensive than in standard courses where students depend on one text and its particular bias for an entire year. The 1990 "Lesbians in Society" course taught by Sharon Stone at Concordia followed in this tradition by offering a series of readings from anthologies and lesbian feminist journals, so that lesbians from the working class, as well as disabled, Asian, Jewish, Black, francophone, Latina, and other lesbians who have traditionally been denied a voice in academia, are heard.

In terms of an extra-curricular presence of lesbians on university campuses, many Canadian post-secondary schools have had lesbian and gay clubs, associations, or gaylines (telephone referral) for years. One example is that of Gays and Lesbians at the University of Toronto (GLAUT) which announced its first meeting in 1969 (then, the Homophile Association) and sponsored its first dance that fall. Events such as Gay Awareness Week, film screenings, and guest speakers from the gay community were, and are still, typical activities for these predominantly social/support groups. It is also typical that the groups were and are gay male dominated. Still, these courageous student groups and their activities represent one of the oldest university affiliated sites of lesbian presence in academe.

In the late 1980s numerous other extra-curricular and extra-institutional resource groups have sprung up for lesbian scholars in Canada. In May 1987 the Lesbian Caucus of the CWSA announced itself and met at the Learned Societies (the annual meeting of many Canadian academic societies) in Hamilton. Encouraging lesbian visibility within the CWSA, within Women's Studies in general and other disciplines, was agreed upon as a basic goal. Fears were expressed that the Learneds were not necessarily a safe place to be spotted as an academic dyke as senior faculty members were often present.[14] There was a discussion on the role of heterosexual women in Lesbian Studies and the role of the caucus within the CWSA. It was decided to ask for a position on the executive to represent the caucus; this was instituted by the following year. In subsequent annual meetings, caucus members brainstormed on what subject matters they could present, inter-disciplinary bibliographies that needed to be compiled, which aspects of Lesbian Studies and which lesbians are particularly absent (Lesbians of Color, francophone lesbians, lesbians with disabilities, etc.), and ways to address these absences in the future. A newsletter from the caucus has appeared sporadically but the annual meetings of the caucus have helped to ensure a continuity of Lesbian Studies presentations and concerns in each CWSA gathering. The 1990 meeting of the CWSA offered no less than nine Lesbian Studies related presentations in their programming.

November 1987 saw the first meeting of the newly formed National Lesbian Forum (NLF) held in conjunction with the annual CRIAW conference (Canadian Research Institute for the Advancement of Women).[15] Twenty-seven lesbians (and women?) attended that first meeting to strategize for an extra-institutional umbrella organization of Canadian lesbian groups, academic and non. Since then, the NLF has met under the auspices of CRIAW and produced a partially bilingual newsletter at irregular intervals. An NLF meeting in Yellowknife in 1989 was particularly exciting as some lesbians living in the North who attended, had never before sat in a room with other lesbians to organize politically.

With the National Lesbian Forum meeting at CRIAW, open lesbians in administrative positions, and the history of Lesbian Studies content in past panels, CRIAW and the CWSA are both providing ongoing forums for lesbians to be visible in academe and Lesbian Studies to be acknowledged and practised.

LESBIAN STUDIES IN UNIVERSITIES ACROSS CANADA

After conducting the Cross-Canada (1987) survey of Lesbian Studies content within Women's Studies, and the rather dismal results, the Lesbian Studies Coalition decided to try another tactic and ask the same schools to send a representative to speak on Lesbian Studies at Concordia University. This turned out to be quite successful as it made the Women's Studies and Women's Centres contacted ask themselves, *who* is doing Lesbian Studies and if no one is, why not? In November 1988, a Cross-Canada Exchange on Lesbian Studies was held at the Simone de Beauvoir Institute. Each representative brought her own viewpoint particular to her position in the institution, be it as student, professor or, in one case, librarian. The results of the exchange, therefore, cannot be seen as a definitive statement on "the" status of Lesbian Studies at that time but more as a series of subjective perceptions and commentaries.[16]

Students from Queen's University (Kingston) and Simon Fraser University (Vancouver) told similar stories of Lesbian Studies being effectively rendered invisible: the difficulty of locating lesbian or lesbian-positive professors, token dykes appearing as guests for the half class devoted to lesbian subject matter, that if any lesbian content were to be presented, they had to do it themselves. The students worried that any Lesbian Studies work they attempted would not be given a sound academic reading and both spoke of being turned into front-line activists in the classroom simply by offering a lesbian perspective.

A student from Ryerson Polytechnical Institute (Toronto), where an on-going series of Lesbian and Gay Studies courses exists, documented the problems of creating a "catch-all" course.[17] The course she attended tried to address a broad audience of lesbophobic straights, lesbians and gays who were just coming out, through to feminist activists; few were satisfied. A practical component where students took placements in local lesbian and gay groups turned out to be very successful.

A staff member from York University (Toronto) compared the development of Women's Studies at York to the potential development of Lesbian Studies. She asked vital questions such as: who do we want teaching Lesbian Studies? and what if there are no "out" professors? A faculty member at Concordia University outlined strategies for integrating Lesbian Studies into Women's Studies courses. Her ideas included reclaiming the generic by considering lesbian experience as *the* human norm, and naming the specificity of heterosexual, white, middle class Women's Studies rather than pretending it is inclusive. Choice of texts proved to be a crucial factor in integrating Lesbian Studies into the mainstream curriculum.

Since the 1988 Cross-Canada Exchange, many changes have

occurred in Lesbian Studies in Canada. It has been reported to the LSCC that for some programs, the exchange acted as a catalyst to action. At Queen's, for example, during the 1989-90 school term, a lesbian speakers series was held and sponsored in part by the Women's Studies department. Students were instrumental in the organizing and the events were well attended. In October 1990, "Justice for All: A Conference on Lesbian and Gay Legal Issues" was sponsored by Queen's Law Lesbians and Gays. The weekend-long event included panels on violence in lesbian relationships, a Native circle, lesbian fertility rights, confronting racial differences, and AIDS, among others. York University held a panel on Lesbian Studies, sponsored by the Women's Studies department, in April 1990. At the University of Alberta, a Lesbian Focus Group developed a non-credit course entitled "Lesbian Visibility/Invisibility" offered through the Faculty of Extension, 1990, to be followed by a course on lesbian sexuality in 1991.[18]

The Simone de Beauvoir Institute has successfully offered a course entitled "Lesbians in Society." Demand for the course was so high that the Institute followed up by offering the same course in the summer. The first ever Lesbian Studies course offered in French in Quebec, entitled "Lesbiennes et Écritures" was to be held in the fall 1990 but was cancelled because of lack of enrolment, and is to be reoffered in fall 1991.[19] "Jewish Lesbians or Lesbian Jews?" was given in January 1991. Taught by an Israeli lesbian, the course began the process of breaking down the dominant WASP discourse which marked many early Women's Studies programs. There is now a commitment to offering ongoing Lesbian Studies courses at one Canadian university—one dream has come true.

Awards and scholarships aimed at encouraging Lesbian Studies, are a natural extension of the burgeoning discipline. In Ontario, a scholarship for lesbians and gay students is now available. The "Bill 7 Award" is named for the Ontario legislation which extended Human Rights protection to lesbians and gays. The Toronto Centre for Lesbian and Gay Studies also offers annual awards to individuals and groups who display a commitment to Lesbian or Gay Studies. In the United States, a Stonewall Scholarship has been created by alumni and current administrators of the University of Chicago Law School for any student who demonstrates "dedication to removing . . . legal and social barriers discriminating against men and women on the basis of their sexual orientation." Naiad Press (a lesbian press) co-sponsors a scholarship with the National Women's Studies Association for a student doing research for an M.A. or Ph.D. dissertation on Lesbian Studies. The Lambda Literary Awards invites you to nominate your favourite Lesbian/Gay book of the year.[20]

In recent publications, *Lesbians in Canada*, edited by Sharon Dale Stone (1990) is an anthology which gathers perspectives from lesbians across the country. Its contents reflect a diversity of lesbian concerns including ageing, the law, motherhood, cultural heritage, lesbians in academe, and geographical isolation. *Resources for Feminist Research* has followed up the 1983 "Lesbian Issue" with an upcoming issue, "Confronting Heterosexuality."

University affiliated Lesbian and Gay Study centers have sprung up at Yale and City University of New York. The Modern Languages Association has a lesbian and gay caucus and the American Educational Research Association also has a Lesbian and Gay Studies Special Interest Group. At the 1990 Harvard conference on Lesbian, Bisexual, and Gay Studies, an informal count of post-secondary schools which offered Lesbian or Gay Studies in some form named over *seventy* institutions in the United States and Canada! And a lesbian sorority, Lambda Delta Lambda, exists at the University of California, Berkeley.

In terms of recording and preserving lesbian history, lesbian archives have been created internationally. The largest and most renowned is that of the New York Lesbian Herstory Archives founded in 1974.[21] It houses a collection of materials: books, photos, letters, diaries, memorabilia, by and about lesbians. The *Archives Lesbiennes* and *Archives Gaies du Québec* in Montreal, and the Toronto Gay Archives and Canadian Women's Movement Archives in Toronto, all hold substantial resources for lesbian researchers.

These are but a few of the recent happenings in Lesbian Studies in Canada and the United States. Lesbian Studies is not just emerging, it is well underway.

LESBIAN STUDIES IN FRANCOPHONE INSTITUTIONS AND ORGANIZATIONS

What seems to be a given trend toward institutionalizing Lesbian Studies in English Canada, has yet to take a toe-hold in francophone academia. Perhaps one of the reasons is that Women's Studies or *Études Féministes* is also less institutionalized. In the fall of 1990, the Université du Québec à Montréal became the first North American francophone institution to offer a Feminist Studies concentration. In terms of Lesbian and Gay Studies, the trend in France is toward "Homosexual Studies," not Lesbian Studies *per se*.

Although francophone universities may lack formal Lesbian Studies courses, individual scholars have produced M.A. and doctoral theses, books, and research papers on Lesbian Studies for decades.[22] In 1988, at the Université de Moncton, a conference was held entitled "Homosexualités et Tolérance Sociale" and the proceedings published.[23]

The same cultural and political pinnings which have made Lesbian Studies possible in anglophone universities have been flourishing in francophone radical lesbian circles. Bookstores, women's centres, journals, theater, the arts, radio, even health services and the bars, have all been sites, at one time or another, of intense intellectual lesbian energy. Journals such as *Amazones d'hier: lesbiennes d'aujourd'hui*, *Treize* and *L'evidente lesbienne* document lesbian political and theoretical thought through to local happenings.[24] Presses which have prioritized publishing lesbian authors, such as *Éditions nbj* (*La nouvelle barre du jour*) and *Oblique Éditrices*, have helped ensure that lesbian culture is kept alive and well.

In the visual arts, *La Réseau Vidé-Elle* has been producing videos which document Quebec lesbian herstory for the past eighteen years. In Montreal theater, *Le Théatre de L'Énergyne* presents plays with lesbian themes and the *Salon des Tribades* has been a site for multidisciplinary lesbian creation. The Montreal women's bookstore, *L'Éssentielle*, which was lesbian owned and operated (it closed its doors in 1991), and *L'Androgyne*, the lesbian and gay bookstore, have both been the site of book launchings and readings for lesbians from Quebec, Canada, and abroad.

In the 1980s, lesbians in Montreal managed a large lesbian/

women's space which, over time, has housed *Traces*, the lesbian archives, a lesbian printer, artists' workshops, a self-defense studio, a lesbian choir and theater troupe, and a large hall for dances and public events. A *Journée d'Interaction* has been held yearly in October which brings together lesbians from across Quebec for workshops, panels, and a stage show.

As with English Canada, the sites for Lesbian Studies in Quebec, Acadia, and elsewhere, have been many and varied. Given the presence of individuals working within the academy, the high profile of Quebec lesbian authors, such as Nicole Brossard or Jovette Marchessault, and a rich francophone lesbian culture already in place, one can speculate that it is only a matter of time before Lesbian Studies will become part of the university curriculum in francophone institutions.

LESBIAN STUDIES–A STUDENT STRUGGLE

Lesbians working within the women's movement or lesbian and gay movement, while still fighting for visibility within these struggles, have come to expect a certain degree of recognition. Some of these lesbians are students and professors and we are now demanding recognition within the academy. Lesbian Studies has to happen, but when and how it will materialize at institutions across the country will very much depend on the individuals present, and often on student activism around the issue. The Lesbian Studies Coalition of Concordia is a case in point. In March 1987, when I first put the two words, Lesbian and Studies together, I hoped, but hardly believed that we would have a series of Lesbian Studies courses at Concordia by 1990.

The Coalition's work has included holding weekly meetings and a bi-monthly discussion/workshop series on topics ranging from "Unlearning Anti-Semitism" to "Lesbian Erotic Images: Bring Your Own." We organize large public events such as the Cross-Canada Exchange, invite speakers like Black American poet Cheryl Clarke, and, in 1991, held an event with Native lesbians. We annually update a *Lesbian Studies Documentation* which includes sample course syllabi, annotated bibliographies, Lesbian Studies awards, etc. We serve a "watch-dog" function for students who report incidents of lesbophobia or heterosexism in their classes or school environment. And, like any feminist group, we are accountable to ourselves to address the needs and rights of lesbians with disabilities, to address racism, classism, anti-Semitism, within our own ranks and when we are aware of it on campus. When we organized a weekend of "Celebrating Lesbians of Color" on the same weekend as the highest Jewish holiday of the year, we were clearly reminded to stay vigilant in maintaining our feminist principles before trying to work elsewhere.

It takes courage, in a male-dominated (and funded) educational system, to defy traditional academic borders by developing new territories of scholarship which directly challenge that system. That a series of Lesbian Studies courses have been held at Concordia attests to an environment in which our hopes and plans could germinate. The principal of the Simone de Beauvoir Institute and individual professors have been instrumental in recognizing the need for Lesbian Studies and finding the flexibility within the existing curriculum to make it a reality. The Institute, in existence since 1978, has made serious efforts at instituting a diverse and representative Women's Studies program. Black Women's Studies, Native Women's Studies and now Lesbian Studies are offered on an ongoing basis.

Members of the Lesbian Studies Coalition of Concordia hope that our example of a student group lobbying for academic change successfully will inspire other students to do the same. We have never looked back. We have never tried to legitimize or explain the need for Lesbian Studies. We explain instead that we are behind the times in not already having a Lesbian Studies degree-granting program in place in Canada. Our motto has been, Lesbian Studies, Ph.D., year 2000! From a 1991 perspective, it doesn't seem so far off . . .

NOTES

1. Questionnaire circulated through Concordia student newspaper, *the Link*, March 24, 1987, conducted by the Lesbian Studies Coalition of Concordia.

2. *Lesbian Studies Documentation* (May 1989 edition), available from the Lesbian Studies Coalition of Concordia, c/o CUSA, 1455 de Maisonneuve West, Montréal, Québec, H3G 1M8.

3. Reported by a Concordia University student to the Lesbian Studies Coalition, 1988.

4. Available from the Lesbian Studies Coalition of Concordia.

5. "Invisible Oppressions: Lesbians at Queen's University," c/o Women's Studies, MacCorry D-514, Queen's University, Kingston, ON, K7L 3N6.

6. 2 Bloor Street West, Suite 100-129, Toronto, ON, M4W 3E2.

7. "Lesbians and Other Women: Integrating Lesbian Studies Into the Women's Studies Curriculum," April 23, 1990, Founders College, York University, Toronto. For an account of the proceedings, contact C.M. Donald, 309 Founders, York University, 4700 Keele Street, North York, Ontario, M3J 1P3.

8. For a summary of proceedings of the Harvard Conference or to contact the above mentioned scholars, write to: Vernon Rosario or Arthur Lipkin, Harvard University, University Hall, Rm B-5, Cambridge, MA 02138. The comments above were taken down in note form at the conference by the author.

9. Despite the achievement of a 6-credit Gay Studies course offered by two tenured professors, this course was given as a one-time Special Topics course and was not re-offered in 1990-91. The Lesbian Studies course, offered within the framework of the Women's Studies program, is ongoing even though the courses are taught by a series of part-time faculty.

10. Communique from the Toronto Centre for Lesbian and Gay Studies, October, 1989.

11. ONE Inc, in Los Angeles, was formed in 1952 as a foundation for teaching and research in Homophile Studies; a library and archival collection was also founded. The pioneering work by the ONE Institute can be seen as "the first crucial stage in the development of lesbian and gay studies in the United States" (Williams,1991).

12. For other early courses taught in Lesbian Studies in the U.S. and the accompanying syllabi, see Cruikshank's, *Lesbian Studies*.

13. A previous attempt at holding a Lesbian Studies course was made by the Simone de Beauvoir Institute (Concordia University) in 1984 but the "Lesbians in Literature" title was changed to "Images of Women's Sexuality in Literature" resulting in confusion for both students and professor. Jeri Wine noted in her Toronto Centre for Lesbian and Gay Studies address (*Rites*, Vol. 6, No. 9, March 1990, p. 12) that she has taught reading courses with "lesbian studies" in the title three times but because they were not "formally constituted" courses, the academy can pretend that Lesbian Studies are not happening. Wine sees the need to go through these formal steps of recognition, as well as the need for "clearly labelled" courses.

14. For details from the first meeting, see the first CWSA Lesbian Caucus newsletter in the CWSA Bulletin, September 1987; also included in the LSCC's *Lesbian Studies Documentation*.

15. NLF, Box 8973, Saskatoon, Sask. S7K 7E7.

16. An entire transcript of the proceedings entitled "Lesbian Studies: A Cross-Canada Exchange, 1988" is available from the LSCC.

17. For information, write to: Ryerson Continuing Education, Ryerson Polytechnical Institute, 350 Victoria St., Toronto, ON, M5B 2K3.

18. For information on this course and subsequent Lesbian Studies courses offered at the University of Alberta, write to: Women's Program, 11019-90 Avenue, University of Alberta, Edmonton, AB, T6G 2E1.

19. It should be noted that, although the "Lesbiennes et Écritures" course was advertised in the regular manner for courses offered through the Simone de Beauvoir Institute, no *special* outreach was done for this first ever French Lesbian Studies course offered at an anglophone institution. The Lesbian Studies Coalition was not notified as to the low enrolment. The loss of the course served to remind the Coalition of the fragility of our gains. In this era when Lesbian Studies are developing, initial efforts within the academy will be strengthened by consultation/coalition with grassroots lesbian groups.

20. For details on any of these listings, see the May 1990 edition of *Lesbian Studies Documentation*.

21. P.O. Box 1258, New York, NY 10116. Tel: (212) 874-7232.

22. A library search for thesis titles pertaining to lesbianism or "female homosexuality" turns up lesbian related topics in practically all francophone universities.

23. Published by the research group *le GRIIGES*; for information write to Les Editions d'Acadie, C.P. 885, Moncton, N.-B., E1C 8N8.

24. *Amazones d'hier: Lesbiennes d'aujourd'hui* (A.H.L.A.), C.P. 1721, Succ. Place du Parc, Montréal, Québec, H2W 2R7; *Revue Treize*, C.P. 771 Succ. C, Montréal, Québec, H2L 4L6; *La Reseau Vidé-Elle*, 4013 rue Des Érables, Montréal, Québec, H3K 3V7; *Traces, Archives lesbiennes*, C.P. 337, Succursale De Lorimier, Montréal, Québec, H2H 2N7.

REFERENCES

Allen, P.G. (1981). Lesbians in American Indian cultures. *Conditions*, 7, 67-87.

Andersen, M.L. (1987). Changing the curriculum in higher education. *Signs*, *12*(2), 222-254.

Bowles, G., & Klein, R.D. (Eds.) (1983). *Theories of women's studies*. New York: Routledge & Kegan Paul.

Cavin, S. (1985). *Lesbian origins*. San Francisco: ism press.

Cruikshank, M. (Ed.) (1982). *Lesbian studies: Present and future*. New York: Feminist Press.

Glasgow, J. (1990). *Gay studies/Women's studies: Natural allies or unnatural bedfellows?* Paper presented at the annual Conference on Lesbian, Bisexual, and Gay Studies, Harvard University.

Grahn, J. (1984). *Another mother tongue*. Boston: Beacon Press.

Gronewold, H. (1990). Helene von Druskowitz's, "Pessimistische Kardinalsätze" (Pessimistic Principles). Presented in "Die geistige Amazone" (The Intellectual Amazon) at the third colloquium on Homosexuality and Literature, Siegen, Germany, October.

Hag Rag (September-October 9987). "Sister News." P.O. Box 93243, Milwaukee, WI, 53203, USA.

Jay, K. (1990). *A lesbian in Boystown: Is this better than the Wizard of Oz?* Paper presented at the annual Conference on Lesbian, Bisexual, and Gay Studies, Harvard University.

The Lesbian Issue (1983). *Resources for Feminist Research, 12*(1).

Lesbiantics (1982). *Fireweed: A Feminist Quarterly.*

Mays, V. M. (1981). I hear voices but see no faces: Reflections on racism and women-identified relationships of Afro-American women. *Heresies* #12, Sex Issue, Vol. 3, No. 4.

Niethammer, C. (1977). *Daughters of the earth: The lives and legends of American Indian women.* New York: Collier.

Raymond, J. (1986). More loose women: The Chinese marriage resisters. In J. Raymond, (Ed.), *A Passion for friends* (pp. 115-145). Boston: Beacon Press.

Rich, A. (1980). Compulsory heterosexuality and lesbian existence. *Signs: Journal of Women in Culture and Society, 5*(4), 631-660.

Stone, S.D. (Ed.), (1990). *Lesbians in Canada.* Toronto: Between the Lines Press.

Williams, W.L. (1991). Letter. *OUT/LOOK*, No. 11, pp. 7-8.

Wine, J.D. (1990). Into the 90s: Lesbian and gay studies in Canada. *Rites*, Vol. 6, No. 9.

Zita, J. (1990). *The Future of Lesbian and Gay Studies: Yet another unhappy marriage?* Paper presented at the annual Conference on Lesbian, Bisexual, and Gay Studies, Harvard University.

History's Future:
Reflections on Lesbian and Gay History in the Community

Will Roscoe, PhD

University of California/Santa Cruz

SUMMARY. From its beginnings in the nineteenth century, the lesbian and gay political movement has been linked to a search for lesbian and gay history. In the post-Stonewall period, community-based historians have been fostering interest in the lesbian and gay past and developing distinctive forms for disseminating their research–in particular, the lesbian/gay archive, the slide-lecture presentation, and the community-based audience. Analyzing the content of these forms reveals how the fascination of the artifact, the image, and the Other fosters the construction of both knowledge and identity. It is these *forms* of knowledge, rather than their content as such, that are in danger of being forgotten as lesbian and gay studies becomes academically institutionalized.

Our history can change the future. When it shows that our presence is not quite so singular; when it reveals fuller images of what

---

As a community-based historian, Will Roscoe has written and lectured widely on the subject of American Indian berdaches. He is the author of *The Zuni Man-Woman* (University of New Mexico, 1991) and the editor of *Living the Spirit: A Gay American Indian Anthology* (St. Martin's, 1988). He has recently breached the boundaries of community and academy and successfully translated his independent work into a PhD in History of Consciousness from the University of California, Santa Cruz.

Thanks are due to Bill Walker, Stuart Timmons, Eric Garber, Harry Hay, Allen Bérubé, and Teresa de Lauretis for comments and assistance.

Correspondence may be addressed to the author at the Institute for Research on Women and Gender, Stanford University, Stanford, CA 94305-8640.

161

it means to be lesbian or gay . . . our history can change the future. And by recovering the past, we make history. Lesbian and gay history is lesbian and gay politics.

* * *

From the beginning, the construction of an identity based on sexual preference has been accompanied by a simultaneous reach into the past, a hasty swaddling of the newborn subject in the cloak of an organic origin. Karl Heinrich Ulrichs, after introducing the subject he called the "Uranian" in his 1864 broadside, *The Vindicator,* proceeded to publish no less than eleven additional treatises that repeatedly dipped into history and anthropology to show, in effect, that his construction was really a discovery. The Uranian was always-already there, in the past of time, in the layers of culture. Edward Carpenter made a similar detour through the archives on behalf of his invention, the "intermediate type." His ethnohistorical treatises, *The Intermediate Sex* (1908) and *Intermediate Types Among Primitive Folk* (1914), have lost none of their charm or originality, and only in recent years has the ethnographic research been improved. In the 1930s, Ruth Benedict, struggling to create her own lesbian lifestyle, succinctly stated the central premise of all these efforts when she wrote, "We have only to turn to other cultures to realize that homosexuals have by no means been uniformly inadequate to the social situation."[1]

At the time, the stakes were enormous. The merest scraps of evidence concerning gay presence in the past or in other cultures could relativize Western values and undermine the argument against homosexuality from nature. Furthermore, given the prevailing mindset of Western epistemology–the conceit that "true" knowledge mirrors nature thanks to the transparency of language–these early activist-scholars could have proceeded no other way. To count as knowledge under Western rules of discourse, knowledge production must erase its tracks.

From the beginning, gay liberation has attracted bookworms, collectors, history buffs, and amateur antiquarians who doubled as activists. In the 1950s and 1960s this included Harry Hay, Dorr Legg, Don Slater, Jim Kepner, Jeannette Foster, Barbara Grier, and Barbara Giddings among others. Lesbian and gay studies were among the first of the "institutionalizations" of the homophile movement–along with the Mattachine discussion group (a vehicle of consciousness-raising) and *ONE Magazine* (a vehicle of education and networking). I find it remarkable that at a time when the rights of homosexuals to free speech and public assemblage had yet to be established, the ONE Midwinter Institute and the *One Institute Quarterly* were founded to provide a forum for such topics as "Berdache and Theories of Sexual Inversion" (Dorr Legg) and "The Moral Climate of Canaan in the Time of Judges" (Harry Hay). It was Hay himself who pinpointed the hold of history on the gay imagination when he referred to this urgent will to knowledge as "the homosexual in search of historical contiguity."

Since Stonewall, the tradition of the activist-scholar has been continued by Arthur Evans, Jonathan Katz, Esther Newton, Vito Russo, John Lauritsen, David Thorstad, Judy Grahn, Allen Bérubé, Joan Nestle, Judith Schwartz, Deborah Edel, Karla Jay, Charley Shively, Paula Gunn Allen, Audre Lorde, Gayle Rubin, Roberta Yusba, Eric Garber, Gloria Anzaldúa, Cherrié Moraga, Joseph Beam, Amber Hollibaugh, Jeffrey Escoffier, and many others. In the 1970s, banners bearing the names of historical gay men and lesbians became a visual cliché in marches and parades, while organizations devoted to gay history formed in many cities. It became possible to speak of a lesbian and gay history movement.[2]

The Buffalo Women's Oral History Project founded in 1978 was among the first of the post-Stonewall history collectives. Its goals are typical: "(1) to produce a comprehensive, written history of the lesbian community in Buffalo . . . ; (2) to create and index an archive of oral history tapes, written interviews, and relevant supplementary materials; and (3) to give this history back to the community from which it derives."[3] This model quickly spread throughout North America.[4] The San Francisco Lesbian and Gay History Proj-2ect, founded in 1979, has been among the most long-lived of these groups. Members of the project were the first to make use of the "slide-lecture" for presenting historical research, beginning with "She Even Chewed Tobacco" (originally "Lesbian Masquerade"), dealing with nineteenth-century women who passed as men, and Allen Bérubé's "Marching to a Different Drummer: Lesbian and Gay Americans During World War II."

These presentations were instant successes. In late 1979 and early

1980, Bérubé toured the East Coast with "She Even Chewed Tobacco," and soon grassroots historians and history projects throughout the country were developing slide documentaries on a variety
of subjects.[5] Today, the slide-lecture is the hallmark of community-
based lesbian and gay history. Taking advantage of a time-honored
"low-tech" medium (the "magic lantern," precursor of the slide
projector, was invented in the eighteenth century), the typical presentation combines a running narrative with the programmed use of
slides. Recorded music and other enhancements are easily added.
The results can approximate the dramatic and visual values of
filmed documentary. Indeed, the use of images in this way enacts
a core metaphor of gay liberation–the shattering of invisibility.

Slide-lectures and the lesbian and gay historians who have trav-
eled throughout the country presenting them deserve much of the
credit for developing the "gay market" that so many book publishers are now eager to infiltrate. The independent scholar, an endan-
gered species in American society at large, has enjoyed a renaissance in the lesbian and gay community. In the past ten years,
unaffiliated lesbian and gay scholars and authors have produced an
impressive number of books, articles, films, and videos without
institutional support–or its corollary, institutional supervision. Their
work has evolved out of close and ongoing interaction with community-based audiences, part of what Lisa Duggan has termed a
"democratic historical practice."

Another important manifestation of community-based history is
the many lesbian and gay archives and libraries that have been
established in North America–over thirty according to a recent
count.[6] In many cases, these archives began as private collections
of books, periodicals, memorabilia or other artifacts. The holdings
of the International Lesbian and Gay Archives in West Hollywood,
for example, grew out of collections started by its founder, Jim
Kepner, as early as 1942. When the collection could no longer be
kept in a private residence–or when two or more collections were
merged (as when two collectors became lovers or one organization
bequeathed its materials to another)–the next step was to "go public." Several of these lesbian and gay archives began as labors of
love on the part of one or two collectors and have remained closely
identified with them (which accounts for both their organizational
stability and their occasional idiosyncrasies).

Today's lesbian and gay archives provide a variety of innovative services. When I visited the Quatrefoil Library in Minneapolis on a rainy Saturday morning in June 1990, I found a small but efficiently organized space staffed by two volunteers and buzzing with a dozen patrons checking out books and videos, conducting research for school papers and other projects, photocopying, and browsing through an international selection of periodicals. David Irwin, cofounder of the library and a self-described "gay bookworm," proudly showed me his latest acquisitions: a collection of rare homoerotic photographs from the 1930s and 1940s and an entire women's lending library donated by a local bookstore.

Similar scenes might be found in San Francisco, Los Angeles, New York, Chicago, Toronto, and many other cities. The International Gay and Lesbian Archives has over 22,000 books, 3,000 periodical titles, and thousands of posters, photographs, artworks, T-shirts, buttons, and memorabilia. The library of ONE, Inc., in Los Angeles, established in the 1950s, has 9,000 volumes and extensive historical files. The Lesbian Herstory Archives in New York, founded in 1974, maintains hundreds of biographical and subject files, several thousand books, over 2,000 slides, and thousands of hours of audio tapes. In San Francisco, the Gay and Lesbian Historical Society of Northern California (formerly the San Francisco Bay Area Gay and Lesbian Historical Society) represents yet another manifestation of the gay history movement. Founded in 1985 as a membership organization "to foster the recovery, preservation, and understanding of the history of lesbians and gay men," the Society sponsors public programs, publishes a newsletter, maintains an office and archives, and regularly interacts with local institutions and libraries.

* * *

In the history of the lesbian and gay movement, it seems that the declaration "Gay Is Good" is always followed by a dash to the library. This dual gesture to future and past is linked to distinctly grassroots politics. Time and again, from the early German emancipation movement to Mattachine and then the Stonewall era, we find activists pursuing history and history being recovered and told in political settings. In North America, the idea of gay and lesbian history and the emergence of a gay and lesbian political movement are so closely linked as to seem inseparable. What characterizes these efforts is not a specific political agenda but the practice of mixing politics and intellectual inquiry in a discourse accessible to a general community.

A merely "historical" account of the gay history movement, however, would miss what may be its most important contribution. This is not the *content* of the works it has produced but the *forms* it has fashioned for disseminating them. These forms—what I refer to as "the artifact," "the archetype," and "the audience"—have been steadily refined since the 1950s. Now, as lesbian and gay studies stand poised for a final assault upon the academy, their future is uncertain. What they represent, the "content of the form" in historian Hayden White's terms, and what is at stake in their preservation is the subject of this paper. To analyze these forms, I will be drawing, somewhat freely, from contemporary cultural theory.

ARTIFACTS AND OBJECTS

In Western civilization, libraries, archives, and museums are key sites for the production of historical knowledge. They are the source of the "raw material"—artifacts and texts gathered from a distance, organized, and made accessible—that historians "process" into historical narratives.[7] It is not surprising that lesbian and gay archives, albeit modest imitations of the great collections of governments and institutions, have been the earliest and most frequent manifestation of the lesbian and gay history movement.

As a cultural form, the archive is above all a collection of objects. Aside from any inscriptions these objects might bear, they are meaningful because they are selected and presented in certain ways. Indeed, in collections the meaning of the relationships between objects often supercedes the individual meaning of the objects themselves. Through exclusion as well as inclusion, by arrangement and organization, collections create a world of values, revealing both personal and cultural ideals of taxonomy, ethics, gender, aesthetics, and so on.

The meaning of *the collection* and *collecting* as cultural forms has been the subject of several recent studies. Historian James Clifford writes that "some form of 'gathering' around the self and the group–the assemblage of a material 'world,' the marking off of a subjective domain which is not 'other'–probably is universal." Collecting produces "rule-governed territories of the self"; it is an exercise in making the world one's own, a mechanism of identity formation.[8] In a similar vein, Susan Stewart writes that "the collection marks the space of nexus for all narratives, the place where history is transformed into space, into property."

What the collection narrates is the self of the collector. As a metaphor of completion, the collection tells the story of the longing for return and reunion with a lost point of origin. For Stewart, this is the mother-infant relationship, and she traces the desire for a "pure object" that "will remain complete at a distance" to the primal disruption of this relationship. Collecting provides a means of objectifying the desire for a nostalgic past, for unity and containment.[9] As Walter Benjamin, an avid book collector, observed, "For the collector–and I mean the real collector, a collector as he ought to be–ownership is the most intimate relationship that one can have to objects. Not that they come alive in him; it is he who lives in them."[10]

The archives of the Gay and Lesbian Historical Society in San Francisco provide a good illustration of how subject and object, desire and history converge in the practice of collecting. According to Bill Walker, long-time steward of the archives, the Society's holdings are characterized by three of its key acquisitions. The first was Walker's own collection of periodicals and publications begun in the early 1970s when he was living in Montana. Collecting gay publications was a way to make political connections through the mail and overcome isolation. A second, key acquisition was the collection of Greg Pennington, a long-time San Francisco resident, who had accumulated clippings, ephemera, and newspapers concerning local history and current events with more of a cultural than a political focus. A third major acquisition was an extensive collection of erotic materials, mostly gay male-oriented, that dated back to the early 1950s. When the collector died, his lover donated the material to the Harvey Milk Archives to prevent it from falling into the hands of nongay relatives; it was subsequently transferred to the Historical Society.

   This last acquisition provides an obvious example of how desire and identity are interwoven in collecting practices. Even before the founding of *ONE Magazine* and the *Ladder* in the 1950s, gay men and lesbians were perusing muscle magazines and lesbian pulp novels.[11] This material was not merely viewed and read; it was, out of necessity as well as desire, hoarded. It became a secret collection. Gay archives, to the extent that their holdings often include such material, quite literally have come "out of the closet." As part of a collection, however, even erotic objects acquire the meta-meanings and metaphors of the *form* of the collection described above. The collection articulates and organizes the nuances of sexual and emotional preference into a kind of erotic personality map; out of this a narrative of the emerging self can be read.

   In this regard, sexual preference plays a much more direct and formative role in identity formation than labelling theory–that prop of social constructionism–allows. It is the objects that desire invests, as much as the labels that society applies, which serve to unleash the flows of signs and meanings, the discursive play, that constitutes and inscribes our subjectivity. As Clifford and Stewart argue, these same processes are at work in all instances of collecting, whether the objects are desired for sexual pleasure or simply to satisfy the collector's compulsion for inclusion and completion. The collection offsets social construction with self-construction.

   We might ask at this point to what extent lesbian and gay collecting reflects the phenomenon Freud termed fetishism. For Freud, the fetish is an object that functions as a substitute for the absent phallus; it sutures the void of castration. In Stewart's terms, the fetish is a "metonymic object" in that it substitutes a signifying object for a part of the body (or a part of the body for the whole). "The boundary between collection and fetishism," she concludes, "is mediated by classification and display in tension with accumulation and secrecy."[12]

   This is a tenuous boundary, but I believe it is both possible and desirable to distinguish fetishism and collecting. While physique magazines and pulp novels, as erotic supplements, can obviously function as fetishes, when they become part of a collection something quite different results. They are no longer merely metonymic objects displacing a transcendental lack (of the phallus, of the maternal relationship). By their placement within a *community* of objects, they begin to function metaphorically and discursively. The collection produces something: it objectifies subjectivity and constructs identity. This is an infinitely more creative function than that of the fetish-object trapped as it is within the closed economy of desire-as-lack. The appropriate metaphor for this capacity, I would argue, is not castration but birth. In other words, what is represented in lesbian and gay collections is not the missing part, but the immanent whole and the process of bringing this into being, which is nothing less than an act of self-birth. Stewart's observation is suggestive. Collecting, she notes, has been "socially placed within the domains of anti- and nonauthority: the feminine, the childish, the mad, and the senile."[13] Might we not add to this list the category of "the queer"?

I hope this discussion suggests how lesbian and gay collections, including collections of fantasy material, can be a rich source of insights into our history, sociology, and psychology. Two examples will illustrate what I mean. In her study of the lesbian pulp novels of the 1950s, Roberta Yusba has shown how a literature intended for the titillation of heterosexual males was subversively written and read by lesbians and how it provided many women, especially in remote areas, a way to begin to articulate their desire.[14] Equally interesting is the psychological reading of gay male erotica by Jungian psychotherapist Robert Hopcke. Hopcke considers erotic narratives a form of folk literature that draws from stock motifs and collective psychological themes. His study reveals that the predominant theme in gay men's erotic literature is that of masculine initiation, enacted between the poles of active/receptive and older/younger (but not masculine/feminine).[15] The narrativization of homosexuality, whether in soft-core lesbian novels or hard-core gay male erotica, interjects a transcendent theme: the production of pleasure becomes a rite of passage.

* * *

Lesbian and gay collecting has played a key role in the history of lesbian and gay identities, communities, and politics. Now, placed in archives, these "objects of identity" are losing their private and purely erotic character. As collective objects, they are being taught to speak and tell stories.[16] But whether private or public, collecting is an indigenous gay practice, continued today by community-based lesbian and gay archives.

ARCHTYPES AND IMAGES

In 1986, I began presenting my research on the subject of the berdache role among the Zuni Indians in the form of a slide documentary.[17] Several months and many presentations passed, however, before I really understood the dynamics of this mode of presentation. This happened when I accepted an invitation to speak to an organization of lesbian and gay business people and professionals in Fresno, California. In San Francisco and Los Angeles, my story of the six-foot tall Zuni Indian We'wha who wore a dress and shook hands with President Cleveland had been enthusiastically received. But how would an audience of lesbian and gay professionals in the middle America setting of Fresno respond to the Zuni "man-woman–as an episode of "gay history"?

In fact, they reacted just as audiences have everywhere–with attention, good humor, and a genuine appreciation of the accomplishments and character of We'wha. A lesbian high school teacher wished her students could see the program for both its Native American content as well as its handling of sex and gender issues. No one complained that I was presenting a stereotype–a dress-wearing man–as a role model.[18]

The next morning, as my lover and I were driving home through the dense winter tule fog of the Central Valley, we marveled over this reception. How was it that diverse audiences responded so well to We'wha's story? At that moment, as the fog literally lifted, I saw the answer. Gay audiences identified with We'wha because they had already identified with his "type" before, in the form of an archetypal figure with innumerable articulations in popular gay culture–the triumphant queen who, being female or identified with the feminine, is powerless in social and economic terms but overcomes all obstacles on the basis of strength of character alone. For my Fresno hosts, a pharmacist and a florist who played us tapes of their favorite show tunes as they drove us home that night, this archetype was no doubt personified by Judy Garland. But its strength and popularity is a function of its adaptability; it can be found not only in the many female figures idolized by gay men, but in the personas of Quentin Crisp, Harvey Fierstein, and Molina in *Kiss of the Spiderwoman*. Whatever form it takes, this figure always tells a "core narrative" of personal redemption through adversity. Thus, in the case of We'wha, no rationalization is needed to convince audiences to take him seriously. In the images of him that I present, his dress juxtaposed to his inherent dignity and self-assurance automatically places him in this category.

But aside from the archetypal content of images, there is the pure fascination and pleasure of viewing them, and this, I believe, accounts for the popularity of slide-lectures in general. *Images,* like collections, clearly have a role in the crystallization of identity. To understand this we need a theoretical orientation that can explain the fascination of the image and its subjective effects, one that I believe Laura Mulvey provides in her article, "Visual Pleasure and Narrative Cinema."[19] Although Mulvey is concerned with the "fascination of film" and how this is "reinforced by preexisting patterns of fascination," I believe the viewing milieu of the slide-lecture–an audience sitting in a darkened room watching larger-than-life images–is similar enough to warrant the use of her analysis.[20]

To explain the appeal of images, Mulvey draws on the theory of French psychoanalyst Jacques Lacan concerning the "mirror stage." This point in infant development occurs when the child first apprehends its own image in a mirror or reflective surface, usually before the age of two. At this stage, the infant still lacks basic motor control–but the image in the mirror appears as an integrated totality, and this gives it irresistible appeal. In Lacan's theory, this primal experience of apprehending one's body-as-an-image is crucial for the constitution of the ego; it is the basis for all subsequent experiences of seeing–and seeking–oneself in others, what Lacan refers to as the "identificatory relations" of the "imaginary," or pre-discursive realm of images.

Mulvey goes on to explore the two forms that pleasure in viewing can take: *scopophilia,* or pleasure in looking at another person as an object, and *narcissism,* the pleasure of seeing oneself in an image, an experience that allows a "temporary loss of ego while simultaneously reinforcing the ego."[21] For Mulvey, the majority of films offer both pleasures in terms of a heroic male figure to identify with and exotic female figures to look at. But for us this raises an interesting question. Which of these pleasures is operative in the case of the gay audience viewing an image it sees as "gay"–say a picture of We'wha, facing the camera, wearing traditional women's clothing but with one arm bare, revealing a pronounced male musculature? Is this scopophilia: seeing the imaged Other as an object of desire and wondering, perhaps, what other physical attributes are beneath that dress? Or is this narcissism: identification with the imaged Other as one's authentic self? It seems to me that in homosexual desire–which is desire for a double rather than an/other–it is impossible to separate scopophilia and narcissism. Lesbians and gay men are able to identify with *and* objectify images, alternately or simultaneously.

But what is the status of these objects-that-are-subjects? Do they provide us with "knowledge" about ourselves or the meaning of the images they appear in? Or are they purely subjective and random? A colleague in gay studies once confessed that he was suspicious of all the slide-lectures because the form itself encouraged anachronistic identifications on the part of the audience. The implication was that such reactions were not only without value, they were counterproductive. And this brings us, fairly abruptly, to the larger question of what counts as knowledge and the debate that opposes positivism to relativism.

Some years ago, R. G. Collingwood, a philosopher of history, proposed a solution to this problem in terms that I think are useful for our purposes. How is it, he asked, if knowledge and thought are strictly context-dependent (the relativist position), we are able to follow the reasoning in the writings of Plato, since his context is lost to us? Collingwood's answer was that thought is more than feeling or sensation, and for this reason it can exist in more than one context without losing its identity, "although without some appropriate context it could never exist." He concludes, "The peculiarity of thought is that, in addition to occurring here and now in this context, it can sustain itself through a change of context and revive in a different one. This power to sustain and revive itself is what makes an act of thought more than a mere 'event' or 'situation.'''[22] To study ideas from the past, therefore, the historian must re-enact them in his or her thought.

The "berdache," following this line of reasoning, is not lost to present-day comprehension, although its original context has lapsed. As an idea–or we might say today a sign or symbol–it can be re-thought by contemporary lesbians and gay men. Such an act is not independent of external factors, however. "The object [of thought] must be of such a kind that it can revive itself in the historian's mind; the historian's mind must be such as to offer a home for that revival."[23] By "home," Collingwood means the contextdependent values, beliefs, experiences, and knowledge of the historian. In other words, neither relativism nor the capacity for cultural comprehension are absolute; but between these two poles a limited domain for critical historical knowledge exists.

An argument like this enables us to see more in the response of lesbians and gay men to historical images than the subjective fantasies of a naive audience. If lesbians and gay men are able to "rethink" the idea of the berdache to the extent of meaningfully responding to it, then there must be an objective basis for this comprehension, some relationship between contexts, experiences, or thought-systems that makes the identification possible. Without this objective basis, identification could not occur–the image would remain alien, incomprehensible. The lecturer might as well be showing slides of Rambo! In other words, it seems to me that the very ability to imagine ourselves in another world and to build conceptual bridges between worlds amounts to a hypothesis of continuity. It is the historian's job to translate such subjective clues into more "objective" knowledge through the use of evidence and criticism.

* * *

The identification of lesbian and gay audiences with historical images and narratives is hypothetical, temporary, and recreational. In the liminal space of the slide-lecture, identities and desires can be tried on. When the program is over, the audience leaves enriched, not converted or programmed. And with the right critical tools, historians can draw valuable insights from these responses into both past and present forms of homosexuality.

AUDIENCES AND OTHERS

An interesting sideline to the history of slide-lectures is the fact that the first of these presentations, on the subject of nineteenth century women, was originally researched by a gay man, Allen Bérubé. Bérubé worked with Estelle Freedman and Liz Stevens to produce the slide-lecture, "She Even Chewed Tobacco," but he delivered the initial presentation himself before a largely lesbian audience at San Francisco's Women's Building in 1979. Bérubé still recalls the trepidation he felt that night, knowing that not only might his research be found wanting, but that his position as a man studying lesbian subjects might be cause for suspicion and resentment. In fact, he received an overwhelmingly enthusiastic response on that occasion and many that followed.

Bérubé's experience is not unique. Eric Garber and myself, both white gay men, have researched African-American and American Indian subjects, respectively. Such cross-cultural investigations by members of a dominant social group have become increasingly problematic in both community and academic settings. To do this kind of research and present it publicly would only seem to invite criticism. But the projects of Bérubé, Garber, and myself have proven feasible for this very reason–their vulnerability to criticism. We have all presented our research directly to the communities affected and were able to complete our projects only because of the cooperation of members of those communities.[24] Consistent and adamant objections, on the other hand, would have brought our efforts quickly to a stop.

The *audience* has a critical role in shaping the production of history, and this is the third "form" of lesbian and gay history that I want to discuss. Setting aside the economic aspect of having an audience (few independent or academic scholars actually earn their living directly from an audience anyway), there are two ways that audiences can influence the production of history. On the one hand, actual (or imagined) experience with audiences can affect the historian's choice and definition of the *subject* and *mode* of presentation, essentially a constraining role. On the other hand, audiences can confirm results, verify evidence, and propose interpretations, which is more of an enabling role. This applies to the production of knowledge in academic settings as well. Academic audiences, whether students, supervisors, funding sources, or peers, enable and constrain research in various ways, according to prevailing values of that world. Scholars, at least those who have been influenced by postmodern critiques of culture and knowledge, would be the first to agree that the difference between knowledge produced in the academy and in the community cannot be characterized in terms of objective or subjective but only by the different rules under which it is produced.

One feature of community audiences, however, has no academic counterpart. In only exceptional instances is the academic setting likely to provide a *predominantly* and *overtly* lesbian and gay audience (indeed, academic audiences in general are rarely inclusive of the populations that academics study). The difference this makes is not in terms of the expertise and interest of a gay audience–for academics have access to interested experts, as well–but in the dynamics that occur when same-sex desire is introjected into historical imagination to produce both knowledge and selves. This is a unique dynamic that can occur only with a lesbian and gay audience.

As we have seen, both objects and images provide access to the imaginary, that primal, pre-discursive domain of images and identifications where the sense of self first develops. The artifact, the archetypal image, and the audience of peers can help create spaces where the imaginary and the real, subjectivity and objectivity, interact. By using these forms, the community historian engages the lesbian and gay imaginary, the wellspring of all identifications, and the source of our desire for "historical contiguity."

This need not be an uncontrolled influence on the production of history. Identification with images in a slide documentary is not purely subjective (or merely objectifying) if the images talk back in the person of the historian and a critical dialogue can unfold. The historian bridges the transition between the imaginary and the real. And while the historian serves as a "reality-check" for audience reactions, the audience can equally check the historian's projections, assumptions, and identifications. This would seem to achieve what Mulvey calls for in regards to narrative film: "to free the look of the camera into its materiality in time and space and the look of the audience into dialectics, passionate detachment."[25]

CONCLUSIONS: HISTORY = LIFE

This inquiry into the forms of the gay and lesbian history movement has led us to humble and unexpected points of origin–magazines hidden beneath mattresses, treasured collections of books and objects, lesbians and gay men peering at slides in darkened rooms–objects and images that not only convey information but shape consciousness and construct identities. In Joan Nestle's words, "Answering the challenge of exclusion is the work of a lifetime."[26] Given all that has been said here, we might give her remark a double reading: Answering the challenge of exclusion is not only work that takes a lifetime, it is work that builds lives and identities, that provides both knowledge of the world and knowledge of the self. It is work that makes lesbian and gay living possible.

In a recent article, Jeffrey Escoffier bemoans the growing hegemony of academic lesbian and gay studies and asks "whether as an academic discipline it should, or can, exist without structural ties to lesbian and gay political struggles."[27] But there is no point in denying that today's out-of-the-closet lesbian and gay academics can improve upon the work of their activist predecessors. This is no comment on the skills of the earlier generation but simply a function of superior resources. Nor is it likely, for the time being, that gay and lesbian scholarship will lose its potential for disrupting the status quo simply because its primary site of production shifts to the campus.

But while the *content* and the *subject* of gay and lesbian studies are likely to remain stable, academic rules of discourse make the future of the *forms* of community-based gay history uncertain. Will the mainstream libraries and institutions now willing to establish lesbian and gay-related collections be as willing to accept erotic or idiosyncratic materials as the community-based archive?[28] Will academically-accountable scholars feel as free to experiment at the borders of objective and subjective knowledge as independent scholars? Will they be as willing or able to engage the imaginary of lesbian and gay audiences?

Escoffier fears that an "unbridgeable gap between gay academics and the community" may result from the institutionalization of gay and lesbian studies. But the potential for disjuncture between scholars and communities always exists, even in the case of the community-based historian. What has bridged this potential gap until now has been the *forms* of community-based knowledge production that I have described here–the collection, the image, and the audience. This is what the lesbian and gay history movement bequeaths to its academic successor–a way to *maintain* a vital link to community.

The lesbian and gay political movement also has a stake in these knowledge-forms. I agree with Escoffier's concern that gay and lesbian history in the future may be produced in forms inaccessible to broad audiences and for audiences other than lesbians and gay men. This bodes ill for the lesbian and gay movement, which, for very practical reasons, needs to have its history constantly retold to avoid having to reinvent its wheels in every generation. While the academic scholar committed to socially responsible professional practice can turn to community-based history for lessons on audience and voice, the activist can gain insights on the power of identity and genealogy to bond and to mobilize.

If the lesbian and gay community-based history movement were to adopt a slogan, it might be simply "History = Life." In the words of the Lesbian Herstory Archives in New York City:

> The Archives doesn't just preserve papers and artifacts. It has honestly preserved Lesbian life and lives, in a hundred small and large ways. The very existence of the Lesbian Herstory Archives, as well as the knowledge contained in those countless files and images, have kept more women going than any of us will ever know. . . . The Archives is where we will be remembered, our writings and images cherished and preserved, our history connected to the future, and our people supported.[29]

NOTES

1. Ruth Benedict, *Patterns of Culture* (Boston: Houghton Mifflin, 1959), 262.

2. See Lisa Duggan "History's Gay Ghetto: The Contradictions of Growth in Lesbian and Gay History," in *Presenting the Past: Essays on History and the Public,* ed. Susan P. Benson, Stephen Brier, and Roy Rosenzweig (Philadelphia: Temple University Press, 1986), 281-90; "Introduction," in *Hidden from History:*

Reclaiming the Gay and Lesbian Past, ed. Martin B. Duberman, Martha Vicinus, and George Chauncey, Jr. (New York: New American Libary, 1989), 1-13.

3. Madeline Davis and Elizabeth L. Kennedy, "Oral History and the Study of Sexuality in the Lesbian Community: Buffalo, New York, 1940-1960," *Feminist Studies* 12(1) (1986): 7-26.

4. These include the New York Lesbian and Gay Historical Society and Lesbian History Project, and the Boston Lesbian and Gay History Project (Duggan, 283-85). While Duggan mentions some activist groups of lesbians and gay men of color with an historical focus, the first minority gay history project that I am aware of is the Gay American Indians History Project founded in 1984 (see Will Roscoe, "Bibliography of Berdache and Alternative Gender Roles Among North American Indians," *Journal of Homosexuality* 14[3/4] [1987]: 81-172; *Living the Spirit: A Gay American Indian Anthology* [New York: St. Martin's Press, 1988]).

5. Other slide-lectures include: Roberta Yusba, "Twilight Tales: Lesbian Paperbacks 1950-65"; Joan Nestle, "Lesbian Courage Pre-1970"; Lesbian Herstory Archives, "Preserving Our Heritage: Issues and Challenges of Doing Lesbian History Research"; Eric Garber, "Tain't Nobody's Bizness: Lesbian and Gay Life in Jazz Age Harlem"; Frances Doughty, "Gilt on Cardboard: Djuna Barnes–Her Life and Visual Art"; Judith Schwarz, "The Radical Feminists of Heterodoxy"; and the Boston Lesbian and Gay History Project, "Our Boston Heritage."

6. The Gay and Lesbian Historical Society of Northern California maintains a current list of these organizations. See also Stuart Timmons, "The Future of the Past: Who Controls Gay History?" *The Advocate,* May 27, 1986: 30-33.

7. This model of "knowledge production" is based on Bruno Latour, *Science in Action* (Cambridge: Harvard University Press, 1987).

8. James Clifford, "Objects and Selves–An Afterword," in *Objects and Others: Essays on Museums and Material Culture,* ed. George W. Stocking, Jr. (Madison: University of Wisconsin Press, 1985), 238, 239.

9. Susan Stewart, *On Longing: Narratives of the Miniature, the Gigantic, the Souvenir, the Collection* (Baltimore: Johns Hopkins University Press, 1984), xii, 125.

10. Walter Benjamin, *Illuminations* (New York: Schocken Books, 1969), 67.

11. The genealogy of this material dates back at least to the 1920s, with the appearance of the first physique magazines and the prototypical lesbian pulp novel, *The Well of Loneliness.* See Roberta Yusba, "Twilight Tales: Lesbian Pulps, 1950-1960," *On Our Backs,* summer 1985: 30-31, 43; "Those Wonderful Lesbian Pulps: A Roundtable Discussion," *San Francisco Bay Area Gay & Lesbian Historical Society Newsletter* 4(4) (summer 1989): 1,4; 5(1) (fall 1989): 7-8; Eric Garber, "'Physique Pictorials': Vintage Beefcake," *San Francisco Bay Area Gay & Lesbian Historical Society Newsletter* 4(2) (winter 1988): 1,7; Michael Bronski, "Art and Evidence," *Gay Community News* (October 21-26, 1990).

12. Stewart, 163.

13. Stewart, xiii.

14. Yusba, "Twilight Tales."

15. Robert Hopcke, *Jung, Jungians, and Homosexuality* (Boston: Shambala, 1989).

16. See Philip Fisher, "The Future's Past," *New Literary History* 6(3) (1975): 587-606.

17. See Will Roscoe, *The Zuni Man-Woman* (Albuquerque: University of New Mexico Press, 1991).

18. I have not encountered the resistance from conservative or "image-conscious" gays that Duggan describes ("History's Gay Ghetto," 288-89), perhaps because audiences are more willing to suspend judgments when it comes to American Indians–a romanticization that I critique in the course of my lecture.

19. Laura Mulvey, "Visual Pleasure and Narrative Cinema," *Screen* 16(3) (autumn 1975): 198-209.

20. Mulvey, 198.

21. Mulvey, 202.

22. R. G. Collingwood, *The Idea of History* (London: Oxford University Press, 1956), 298-99, 301, 297.

23. Collingwood, 304.

24. For an account of my experience lecturing at the Pueblo of Zuni, see Will Roscoe, "The Zuni Man-Woman," *Out/Look* 1(2) (summer 1988): 56-67. For a discussion of Garber's work, see Duggan, "History's Gay Ghetto," 287.

25. Mulvey, 209.

26. Joan Nestle, *A Restricted Country* (Ithaca, NY: Firebrand Books, 1987).

27. Jeffrey Escoffier, "Inside the Ivory Closet: The Challenges Facing Lesbian & Gay Studies," *Out/Look* 3(2) (fall 1990): 40.

28. See Bill Walker, "Evaluating the Current Status of Lesbian and Gay Archival Collections," unpub. ms., 1989; Timmons, "The Future of the Past."

29. *Lesbian Herstory Archives Newsletter* #11 (January 1990), [insert].

APPENDIX

Excerpts from *In Every Classroom: The Report of the President's Select Committee for Lesbian and Gay Concerns*, Rutgers University
Permission to reproduce part of Nieberding, R. A. (Ed.) (1989), *In Every Classroom: The Report of the President's Select Committee for Lesbian and Gay Concerns* (New Brunswick, NJ: Rutgers, The State University), is granted by the President's Select Committee for Lesbian and Gay Concerns, Rutgers, The State University. The excerpts are reproduced from pp. 8-10, 20.

Printed copies of *In Every Classroom: The Report of the President's Select Committee for Lesbian and Gay Concerns* are available for $10.00 each from: The President's Select Committee for Lesbian and Gay Concerns, 301 Van Nest Hall, Old Queens Campus, Rutgers University, New Brunswick, NJ 08903. Checks are to be made payable to Rutgers, The State University.

Executive Summary

STRUCTURE AND HISTORY

Rutgers University President Edward J. Bloustein announced the creation of his Select Committee for Lesbian and Gay Concerns on February 3, 1988. The Committee is part of the University's larger commitment to combatting prejudice and encouraging respect for diversity, known as the Program to Advance Our Common Purposes. The Select Committee was created in response to recommendations made by lesbian and gay students and the Rutgers Sexual

Orientation Survey completed under the direction of Dr. Susan Gavin. Both the students and the survey documented a homophobic atmosphere that the survey's report described as "a vicious, sometimes violent underside to life here at Rutgers."

Chaired by Dean James D. Anderson, the Select Committee is composed of twenty-nine members, including faculty, students, administrators, and alumni. The Committee organized itself into nine task groups and held a total of 71 meetings on the Camden, Newark, New Brunswick, and Piscataway campuses, including three Open Forums. In addition to the Calvin study, which documented homophobic violence, four other surveys were completed: a lesbian and gay student needs assessment survey; a survey of all faculty and staff on work environment and curricular issues; a survey of campus resources and programs available for lesbian and gay students; and a national survey of lesbian and gay programs and projects underway at other colleges and universities.

The Select Committee for Lesbian and Gay Concerns examined a number of areas where the University routinely interacts with students, faculty, and staff in ways which significantly affect the quality of their personal lives, their education, and their work. The Committee examined areas where heterosexism is currently institutionalized, and areas where homophobia, anti-gay violence, and discrimination can be aggressively combatted. Our recommendations are made with the assumption that heterosexism and homophobia, like racism and sexism, are long-term problems which demand long-term solutions. As a result many of our recommendations are designed to be implemented over a period of time. However, some key recommendations need urgent action if the University is seriously to oppose and tackle bigotry, prejudice, and discrimination against lesbian and gay people. The following overview summarizes the most pressing recommendations, those recommendations which the members of the Select Committee for Lesbian and Gay Concerns feel need the most immediate and serious action.

GOALS OF THE SELECT COMMITTEE

The Select Committee's work has been guided by four goals or assumptions. They represent the spirit of our work and have guided the drafting of our recommendations. We hope they will guide the implementation and refinement of our recommendations as well.

First and most important, the University must ensure an environment in which all members of our community, and specifically gay and lesbian students, are able to participate and develop intellectually and emotionally, free from fear, violence, or harassment. For most students, college is a time of self-exploration, a time when personal identity and independence are solidified and asserted. For lesbian and gay students it is too often a period of personal turmoil and isolation as they come face to face in their daily lives with the ugliness of homophobia and heterosexism. Since a primary mission of the University is to educate its students, it is critical to provide them with the chance to grow and learn in a safe environment free of homophobia and heterosexism. No one–of whatever race, gender, religion, color, national origin, ancestry, age, physical ability, *or* sexual orientation–should be subjected to physical threats or abuse, academic depreciation or intellectual derision, or to treatment which deprives them of their dignity and humanity. Any community which does not aggressively work to protect its members from the physical, emotional, and intellectual ravages of bigotry and prejudice is a community for which freedom of expression and intellectual integrity are a farce.

Second, the University needs to promote a respect for diversity among all its members. It must combat homophobia and heterosexism as an essential part of that effort. Both the bigot and the bigot's prey are injured by prejudice and hate. Both parties lose the opportunity to participate in honest discussion; neither can share their knowledge and insight; everyone's growth and richness of experience is stunted. The bigot's hate is exhausting and depleting for everyone; as Frederick Douglass said, "Slavery enslaves the slave-master as well." A truly exciting intellectual environment is one which celebrates its own diversity and rich complexity, not one which sulks in fear of what it cannot easily understand or what it cannot conquer and make its own.

Third, the University must ensure equitable and fair treatment for all members of the Rutgers community–students, faculty, staff, administrators, alumni, and their families. Equity is a central tenet of the American creed, enshrined in our nation's founding documents. Fairness must be understood within the context of the diversity and difference which currently exists within our communities. What is often seen as offering the same benefit or service equally to all members of the community may actually be exclusionary when viewed from the perspective of one part of our diverse world. For the University to offer all married couples spousal benefits and claim equality of treatment is to disavow the existence and ignore the history of lesbians and gays who are denied the legal option of marriage in all countries but Denmark.

Finally, the University needs to encourage research and scholarly debate in the areas of lesbian and gay studies. Society needs to understand the roots of heterosexism; we need to understand why the assumption of heterosexuality is so pervasive and firmly rooted in our thought (Rich, 1980) and why all forms of same-sex intimacy are so frightening and threatening to so many people. Solving the problems of bigotry will require thorough research and serious scholarship. If lesbian and gay people are to become full participants in public life, society must be allowed to discover the contributions that lesbians and gays have made to science, history, literature, and art; they need creative research which allows them to recover and create the science, history, literature, and art which is their own.

FIVE FUNDAMENTAL OBJECTIVES FOR RUTGERS

The Select Committee sees five objectives as central to accomplishing its goals. After examining the research and surveys we commissioned, after participating in a University-wide dialogue and numerous meetings, we believe that these objectives provide the best strategy for implementing the principles just outlined. The following five objectives deserve the immediate attention of the University.

1.   *The establishment of an Office for Lesbian and Gay Concerns with at least one full-time staff person.*

A central University Office provided with staff and resources and advised by a committee of faculty, staff, students, and alumnae/i is needed to provide a visible, prominent focus for the long-term work of implementing this report's recommendations. Someone is needed to act as a voice for the issue who is undistracted by other necessary concerns and complicated problems which currently confront university administrators; at least one person needs to have ultimate responsibility for responding to specific problems or incidents. At present, responsibility for combatting homophobia is shared by everyone and held by no one. A full coordinator would act as a gentle reminder of what needs to be done, what hasn't been done, and what should be done. Also, a professional is needed with the skills, expertise, and time to serve as a clearinghouse for effective strategies and creative programs for change and to prevent duplication of efforts across the University.

2. *The creation of incentives for the interaction of the "new curriculums."*

Scholarship and learning are expanding as new social groups with new experiences, different cultures, and unexplored histories take their place in our public life. Some of the most exciting and innovative scholarship, especially at Rutgers, is interdisciplinary work taking place within such new arenas as women's studies, Africana studies, American studies, and lesbian and gay studies. These emerging areas of scholarship, these "new disciplines," need to be better integrated into our existing teaching curricula and our standard pedagogy.

This can only be done through the allocation of new resources by the University to support and encourage the development of "new curriculums" that are inclusive of not just the lesbian and gay experience, but also of other under-represented groups. Incentives, such as release time or rewards in the tenure and promotion process, must be created so that faculty members who take time from their current teaching, research, and service to revise the curriculum they teach are not penalized in the tenure and promotion process. Faculty members who are doing creative research in these areas and who are developing inclusive curriculums need to be provided forums, such as discipline-based colloquia, for sharing these advances with their colleagues.

The inclusion of lesbian and gay people in the intellectual discourses of the classroom is crucial to combatting homophobia and heterosexism, since it demonstrates the intellectual and academic legitimacy which lesbian and gay issues deserve.

3. *Combatting homophobia through distinct, tailored sensitivity programs.*

We must develop programs and educational activities in a variety of formats on homosexuality, lesbianism, bisexuality, and hetero-sexism on all campuses, particularly for new students during orientation; for students in residence halls, fraternities, and sororities; and for faculty, administrators, and staff, especially in such areas as health care, campus security, residence life, and counseling–the entire student life area in general.

Anti-homophobia education and training can be integrated into existing anti-bias activities throughout the University, especially as they relate to other forms of prejudice such as racism, sexism, xenophobia, and prejudice directed towards members of religious or national groups.

4. *The creation of safe space.*

All public space at the University should be safe space free of racist, sexist, anti-Semitic, and homophobic bigotry. This is an ambitious project which will take many years to achieve. However, until the time arrives when two women or two men can safely walk arm in arm through campus and show their affection for each other publicly, as so many opposite-sex friends do, we need to create a space where lesbians, gays, bisexuals, and their friends can interact and develop supportive communities. We need to protect the vulnerable for now. We are not suggesting the creation of an exclusive space, just space free from harassment and hostility.

5. *Ensure equity in access to benefits and services.*

Currently lesbians and gays are denied access to benefits and services which are in principle said to be supplied to all employees. The most egregious and serious example of this exclusion is in the area of employee health benefits. Until the University provides equal health insurance benefits to the domestic partners and children of lesbian and gay employees it is not meeting the requirements of its own nondiscrimination policy.

REFERENCE

Rich, A. (1980). Compulsory heterosexuality and lesbian existence. *Signs*, 5, 631-660.

Faculty Reading:
Suggestions for Teaching

The Survey of All Faculty and Staff included an open-ended question which asked teaching staff to list "any articles, books, etc. about the lesbian or gay male experience that you have found helpful in addressing these issues in your teaching." Here are a few of their suggestions:

Altman, Dennis. *The Homosexualization of America, The Americanization of the Homosexual.* New York: St. Martin's Press, 1982.

Avicolli, Tommi. "He Defies You Still: The Memoirs of a Sissy," *Radical Teacher* # 24 pp. 4-5. Also in *Men Freeing Men*, Francis Baumli, ed. Atlantis Press.

Cruikshank, Margaret, ed. *Lesbian Studies: Present and Future.* Old Westbury, NY: Feminist Press, 1982. Includes the article "Sample Syllabi and Courses in Lesbianism."

de Beauvoir, Simone, *The Second Sex.* New York: Vintage Books, 1952/1974. Includes the chapter, "The Lesbian."

Boswell, John. *Christianity, Tolerance and Homosexuality: Gay People in Western Europe from the Beginning of the Christian Era to the Fourteenth Century.* Chicago: University of Chicago Press, 1980.

Clarke, Cheryl. "Of Althea and Flaxie" *Narratives: Poems in the Tradition of Black Women.* New York: Kitchen Table: Women of Color Press, 1982.

de Lauretis, Teresa. *Technologies of Gender: Essays on Theory, Film and Fiction.* Bloomington: Indiana University Press, 1987. Also *Alice Doesn't: Feminism, Semiotics, Cinema.*

Dinnerstein, Dorothy. *Mermaid and the Minotaur: Sexual Arrangements and Human Malaise.* New York: Harper and Row, 1976.

Dover, Kenneth J. *Greek Homosexuality,* Cambridge, MA: Harvard University Press, 1978.

D'Emilio, John. *Sexual Politics, Sexual Communities: The Making of a Homosexual Minority in the United States, 1940-1970.* Chicago: University of Chicago Press, 1983.

Duberman, Martin Bauml. *About Time: Exploring the Gay Past.* New York: Gay Presses of New York, 1986.

Faderman, Lillian. *Surpassing the Love of Men: Romantic Friendship and Love Between Women from the Renaissance to the Present.* New York: William Morrow, 1981.

Fricke, Aaron. *Confessions of a Rock Lobster.* Boston: Alyson Publications. 1981.

Foucault, Michel. *The History of Sexuality: Vol. 1: An Introduction.* Translated from French by R. Hurley. New York: Pantheon, 1978.

Grahn, Judy. *Another Mother Tongue: Gay Words, Gay Worlds.* Boston: Beacon, 1984.

Grier, Barbara. *The Lesbian in Literature.* 3rd ed. Tallahassee: Naiad Press, 1981.

Herdt, Gilbert. *Guardians of the Flutes: Idioms of Masculinity.* New York: McGraw-Hill, 1981.

Lorde, Audre. *Zami: A New Spelling of My Name.* Trumansburg, NY: Crossing Press, 1983.

Leavitt, David. "Territory" in *Family Dancing.*

McDaniel, Judith. "Is There Room for Me in the Closet?" in

Gendered Subjects: The Dynamics of Feminist Teaching, Culley and Portuges, eds. Routledge and Kegan Paul, 1985.

Moraga, Cherrie, and Gloria Anzaldua (Eds.). *This Bridge Called My Back: Writings by Radical Women of Color*. Watertown, MA: Persephone Press, 1981.

Newman, Leslea. *A Letter to Harvey Milk*. Ithaca: Firebrand Books, 1988.

Morrison, Toni. *Sula*.

Narayan, Uma. "Working Together Across Differences," in *Social Work Processes*. Also in *Hypatia*, Summer, 1988.

Plato. *The Symposium*.

Pratt, Minnie Bruce. "Identity: Skin, Blood, Heart" in *Yours in Struggle: Three Feminist Perspectives on Anti-Semitism and Racism*. Elly Bulkin, Minnie Bruce Pratt and Barbara Smith, eds. Brooklyn, NY: Long Haul Press, 1984.

Renault, Mary. *The Persian Boy*.

Rich, Adrienne. "Compulsory Heterosexuality and Lesbian Existence," in *Women, Sex, and Sexuality*. Catharine R. Stimpson and Ethel Person, eds. Chicago: University of Chicago Press, 1980. Also *The Dream of a Common Language* and *On Lies, Secrets and Silence*.

Roberts, J. R. *Black Lesbians: An Annotated Bibliography*. Tallahassee: Naiad Press, 1981.

Sedgwick, Eve Kosofsky. *Between Men: English Literature and Male Homosexual Desire*. New York: Columbia University Press, 1985.

Smith, Barbara, ed. *Home Girls: A Black Feminist Anthology*. New York: Kitchen Table Press., 1983. Also *But Some of Us Are Brave*.

Smith-Rosenberg, Carroll. "Female World of Love and Ritual," *Disorderly Conduct: Visions of Gender in Victorian America*. New York: Alfred A. Knopf, 1985.

Stein, Gertrude. *Melanctha*.

Walker, Alice. *The Color Purple*.

Wittig, Monique. "The Straight Mind," *Feminist Issues* (Summer 1980), pp. 105-6.

Wittig, Monique. *The Lesbian Body*. Boston: Beacon Press, 1973/1986.

Woolf, Virginia. *Mrs. Dalloway.*

Zimmerman, Bonnie. "What Has Never Been: An Overview of Lesbian Feminist Literary Criticism," *Signs* 9 (1984), pp. 663-82. Also "Exiting from Patriarchy: The Lesbian Novel of Development."

Also recommended were such *films* as Pink Triangles, Before Stonewall, Torch Song Trilogy, On Being Gay, A Special Place, Word is Out, In the Best Interests of the Children, and We are Family.

Index